ON THE PATH OF THE BELOVED

ON THE PATH OF THE BELOVED

By Leslie Brooks

with Mary Magdalen and Others

ON THE PATH OF THE BELOVED
Copyright © 2014 by Leslie Brooks

All rights reserved.

For information about permission to reproduce selections from this book,
write to: Permissions, Love Incarnate Books,
Post Office Box 111, Colrain, Massachusetts 01340

Book design by Robin Brooks, The Beauty of Books
Production by Love Incarnate Books
Typeface, Perpetua
Cover Drawing by Leonardo da Vinci

Published 2015
21 20 19 18 17 16 15   1 2 3 4 5

ISBN 978-0-9966523-0-8
Library of Congress Control Number: 2014909780

Published by Love Incarnate Books
www.love-incarnate.com

To all beings,

with love,

delight,

and expectancy

TABLE OF CONTENTS

ACKNOWLEDGMENTS xi

INTRODUCTION xiii

PART ONE — *A Birth Mother Dies*

    1. THE RED ROOM 3

    2. MOTHER DARKNESS 11

    3. I, MAGDALEN 17

    4. AFTER MAGDALEN 33

    5. FLAME OF CREATION 37

    6. THE HIDDEN SOURCE 47

    7. RELEASING THE KARMIC BARGE 61

    8. ALLOW YOUR SMALLNESS 75

    9. ALLOWING LOVE IN 85

    10. LOVING MOTHER WITHIN 91

    11. JUST FEELING 105

    12. TRANSMISSION OF LOVE 111

PART TWO — *Moving, Deconstruction, Renovation*

13. MOTHER OCEAN *123*
14. ONCE UPON A TIME *127*
15. BATTLE OF THE VEILS *135*
16. VISITATION *145*
17. CASTLE IN THE MISTS *149*

PART THREE — *Magic Returns*

18. KEEPER OF THE LAND *159*
19. HONORING THE SELF *163*
20. NOTHING TO FORGIVE *167*
21. MY MOTHER'S MOTHER'S MOTHER *173*
22. UNDER THE ANCIENT ONE *175*
23. IMPATIENCE OF A MASTER *179*
24. THEY WHO LIGHT THE EARTH *189*
25. ON THE PATH OF THE BELOVED *201*
26. THE DIVINE FEMININE *205*
27. THE "SIN" OF OBESITY *211*
28. BODY BELOVED *225*
29. THE SUBSTANCE OF JOY *237*
30. ALTARS TO THE BELOVEDS *247*

EPILOGUE *251*

NOTES *257*

GLOSSARY* *261*

SELECTED BIBLIOGRAPHY *269*

---

*Note to Readers: Some names and terms in this book are accompanied by a superscript [G]. Kindly refer to the *Glossary* for their meanings.

ACKNOWLEDGMENTS

I lovingly thank Anjee Uprichard for reading every new edit with support and delight, and for daring to share her inner galaxy with me.

I thank my identical twin Robin for choosing, as soul, to share this lifetime with me so that I would not, this time, be alone on this path. I also thank her for all her loving and patient support in designing this book.

I thank Moriah Marston for all of the ways in which she has enhanced my path to ensoulment.

I thank my editors Ann McNelly and Frances King for their impeccable patience and kind, loving, and wise suggestions.

And of course, I thank all of the Beloveds, in all forms you take!

—— *Leslie Brooks*

INTRODUCTION

January 20, 2012, Colrain, Massachusetts

My mother died in 2009. Afterwards, I felt lost and ungrounded, and found myself searching for "mother" in home and in self.

I've known how to build, accomplish, create, channel, manifest, and do many things, but I have never really known how to love and nurture myself, treat myself as a beloved, body and soul. What would that look like?

The name for this book came to me years ago, as if from some deep unconscious longing within my soul. But what does it mean "to walk the path of the beloved"? Who or what is "the beloved"? How do I write about the beloved when I don't even know what it is?

Somehow, I know that loving oneself is an integral quality of the divine feminine, but what is "the divine feminine"? How have

I, as a spokesperson—a spokeswoman—for the collective consciousness,[G] learned to deny, shame, criticize, and minimize that which is the Sacred within me? (Words that bear the superscript[G] are defined in the *Glossary* in the back of this book.)

As I began to think about this book, I began to trace back to my childhood for the origins of my own issues around the feminine within me. I remembered that, after her first child, a boy, was born, my mother miscarried a second boy whom she named Philip, for whom she grieved all of her life. After that miscarriage, she gave birth to my identical twin sister and me.

In unspoken ways, she turned to me to replace Philip. She named me after Leslie Howard, one of her favorite male actors from the 1930s. She dressed me in blue, a "boy color," while my twin was dressed in red or pink, to distinguish us from each other. When my twin and I were given twin dolls, I got the boy doll.

My mother appointed my twin "eldest daughter" so that, even though she was only eleven minutes older, she actually babysat me! Partly because of all this, and partly because of my own particular soul path, I learned to deny the feminine in myself.

As I explored the meaning of "beloved" for this book, I realized I wanted to develop a loving mother within, and that doing so was the first step in treating myself as beloved. I began to explore the concept of the divine feminine, what that was, and what it might mean to me, as a way of helping me find the feminine, the Mother, in myself.

For assistance in this exploration, I mostly turned to the ascended master^G Mary Magdalen with whom I have had a relationship for many years. I see her as not only a best friend and wife to Yeshu (Jesus), but also a teacher, prophet, healer, and ascended master in her own right. In this book, when I call her "The Magdalene," she is a teaching energy often speaking for the divine feminine or the Mother. When I call her "Magdalen," she is the person she was with Yeshu who is also now an ascended master.

I will try here to describe how I see the ascended masters. They are beings that are no longer in body (incarnate), having completed (mastered) all of their souls' lessons and issues so that they are now "ascended," which means risen to Heaven. I see them as sitting in the masters' hall, at the right hand of what I call Source, the source of all love and light, and all things, all beings.

Their task as I see it is to assist all beings in completing our souls' karmic issues^G so that we too may ascend or, if we wish, continue to come back into body to teach and assist others. I believe in past lives and I believe that my role in this and many lifetimes has been to teach and assist others, as well as to continue to learn and advance myself. The masters are also here to love, hold, and support us on our individual journeys, in all ways. They are always available to us.

Source, the source of all things, is also with me always, and with all beings. Others may have other words for this Great

Love, such as God, Creator, Spirit, Allah. Replace the word if you wish, or not.

The magic of the multidimensional^G realm and the masters have been with me for most of my life. At first, as a child in the crib, I felt the elementals^G of the wind, rain, starlight, trees and plants, as if they were best friends and allies. They offered me support and delighted me with their humor and love. Later, as an adult, I connected with the masters, calling them "Sweet Ones."

Now, I call them "the Beloveds," capitalizing the "B." When referring to the precious intimacy of discovering the beloved in myself, as well as all others on this path, I use the lower case "b." The masters refer to me in the same intimate way. From a place of mystery deep inside of me, the spellings feel exactly right.

In the first part of this book, I call on several masters to help me in my voyage of discovery, as I search for answers to questions that I believe are asked now by the collective consciousness, as it endeavors to evolve all humanity to a multidimensional presence that includes all beings in all universes.

Multidimensionality is a state of going beyond what we know in our three-dimensional world, allowing our sixth and other senses to grow and expand until we remember the time of living with the angels, the time when we were Source, before Source created us as sparks of itself to learn more. The soul is a multidimensional part of ourselves, for it has lived many lifetimes and not always in human body, or even in body at all.

The way that I access the masters is by what many call "channeling." What that means to me is that I connect with a higher part of myself, what I call my "Source Self," by means of a simple induction (see p. 48, starting with "I call forth the pure white crystalline light...") and my intention. I then call on whoever I think would best answer the question or issue, or whoever's presence I feel "coming in." It is somewhat like sensing the presence of a person in the room, even though he or she is making no sound and is behind you, or out of view. In this book, I am referred to as "the channel."

Really, anyone can channel. I once took a ten-day workshop in which we were told that by the end of it, we had to be able to channel. Of course, I was terrified that I couldn't do it. I was not in the room when the teacher rescinded this requirement, and I found that I could and did indeed do it anyway! It is really about allowing for the unknown, inside or outside of us, to speak, and believing that what comes is true. Whether imagined or real, I know that what comes does not come from the personality me, the three-dimensional me.

I recorded many of the transmissions in this book, via microphone, directly into recording software on my laptop, and then I burned them onto CDs so I could listen to them again. In some cases, I have included my induction in the text, to strengthen the reader's access to the feeling of the channeling.

Some readers may wish to imprint a transmission, especially the very loving ones, in a more personal way. I would suggest selecting whatever fits for you out of the words, maybe adding your own or changing them somewhat to make them your own. Then record the transmission in your own voice so that you can embed it more deeply into you and listen to it again and again.

This is completely up to you, the reader, and it is a way of loving yourself to ask what is right for you alone.

Towards the second half of this book, I realized that I did not always need to ask the masters to speak for me. I found that I could call on my own ascended master self, my Source Self, as I move, more and more, into the master self that I am becoming. Is this not the time for all of humanity to move into its mastery? When I have asked myself how I dare to share my descents as well as my heights, I continue to hear, *It is the path as it unfolds.*

I have chosen to put both the words of the masters and other beings, and also my own words when speaking to them, into *italics* for ease of flow. Also, there are times when I use *italics* to heighten the magical quality of the words for my readers.

Much of this writing, the wisdom parts of it, you may already know or remember, from the time when we were truly One with Source. There is no hierarchy here. Your presence is as implicit as it is necessary, for the words to come. The story, which weaves its way through the book, is mine but I offer it to you as yours, as I believe that we have all lived or will live, at one time or another, each other's story.

I have chosen the image on the cover to represent the innocence, as well as the unconscious beauty of a young woman. It is Leonardo Da Vinci's *La Scapigliata*,[1] which means, literally, "disheveled." It is named so because it is an unfinished sketch of the Madonna done for an Italian noblewoman.

This is how I feel myself to be, as I begin this book: unfinished, a sketch of who I want to be, of what I want to learn. She is also perhaps Magdalen. Perhaps she is the divine feminine, unformed, unnamed, unknown. Perhaps she is an exploration into the unknown of her own inner self, as well as into the ongoing mystery of this new consciousness that lives within our individual Source Selves.

I now hand the questions and the answers over to the multidimensional I-AM-ness that I have become, knowing that by the end of this journey, I will understand what it means to "walk the path of the beloved."

Perhaps this writing will assist in your own inner unfolding, dear readers, whether you be man or woman, boy or girl, or other being.

As you intend it, so does it happen.

Allow also that the intention may transform, as you do.

I offer to you, with this writing, my love, my joy, my gratitude, and my delight in each of your own voyages, as you travel the path of the beloved that you are.

PART ONE

A Birth Mother Dies

1

THE RED ROOM

August 2, 2009

My mother died January 30th.

That morning, I felt called to read the 23rd Psalm[2] to her, as well as a passage from *Love Incarnate*,[3] my first published book. I found her Bible, got my book, and went up to her room where she lay in the hospital bed provided by Hospice.

The half hour I spent with her around her death was one of the most profound and beautiful experiences of my life. Thinking she was asleep, I kissed her on the forehead, and held her little hand, still warm, and began to read. Halfway through the psalm "The Lord is my Shepherd…," I noticed that her carotid artery was still and that she was no longer breathing, and I realized that she had passed just before I arrived in the room.

I finished the psalm and then, with deep awe and devotion, I began to read from the place in *Love Incarnate* where Yeshu moves to the light just after his death, knowing that she was there also.

I include the passage here so that you, dear readers, may share in that time with me.

> *There is no wall or boundary between beings. There is only Love that joins us, and understanding, and Joy. And I already feel myself hovering above my body.*
>
> *I tell you now I feel the Great Love coming here (tears of Joy in his voice). I feel myself gently lifting. I hear the flutter of the wings of angels. I hear the beautiful ethereal voices of the angelic realm singing. It is a beautiful passing. It is a beautiful journey. I see such great Light. I feel such great Joy!*
>
> *My Heart, there is no room in my body for this Heart that sings, that Joyously embraces, that is embraced in this Great Love, this great Joy!*
>
> *I feel myself moving through streams of lifetimes, through streams of angelic realms, etheric realms…of all lifetimes, all peoples, all souls streaming by, like a stream of meteors flowing through and around me on either side! It is as if the Light of my Joy, my Light, my very Being, goes out to the far corners of the universe, to all universes!*
>
> *Human eyes could not possibly contain this Light! A human Heart could not contain this Joy!*
>
> *I rest. I rest in this Light and in this Joy, in the bosom of my Father, my Mother / Father / GOD / Great Love.*

There is so much that I would learn! There is so much that I would tell! And yet, there are no words for the telling of this Joy.[4]

Because I knew that place, had experienced it through him, I was there with my mother too. It was as if the three of us shared that time. The joy in the room, and the light, were palpable. I could not help feeling blessed by it, in a state of grace.

Later, I found myself torn between the loss of the loving being that my mother had become in the last two months of her life, and my rage at the woman who had birthed me but never nurtured me. The only thing that was real for me was that treasured halo of time that I had shared with her just after her death.

After the funeral, it was up to us "children" to empty my mother's house, a big New England colonial with a library that went back to 1776. I wanted to throw out the junk, in order to heal the structure of the house, as a way of clearing and healing the "junk" of a painful childhood out of my own psychic structure.

My attempts to help were rejected by the sibling in charge because she assumed I wanted to throw out everything, which was not true. I was banned from my childhood home. The only thing left to my psyche was to turn to my own home instead.

I found myself wanting to create a room in my basement where I could be in the dark, away from the bright, light-filled space that is the rest of my house. I wanted to curl up and suck my thumb and sleep and sleep and sleep.

Because I have always been an artist, I learned to use tools at an early age. So, it was not difficult logistically to manifest what I was driven to create in that basement room. I painted the walls a warm dark grey, and draped them with cloth of sheer rich burgundy, sculpted with moss-colored velvet. I covered the concrete floor with oak-patterned flooring. I bought a deep red satin comforter with dark red sheets, and dark red satin shams with gold threads, and throw pillows the color of fire and blood. I placed a black velvet cloth sculpted in runes on a dark oak table and created an altar there, with candles and shells and stones from my land. A black electric fireplace added the element of fire and warmth.

I didn't know what I was doing. I just knew I had to do it. I wept when I couldn't find the right thing, or when I couldn't get it right, just as I wept as a child when I needed a mommy and didn't have one, because she couldn't get it right either.

When it was all done, after weeks of preparing the room and myself, as if for an initiation, I put on my jammies, closed the door, lit the candles, climbed inside the blood red sheets, and breathed a deep sigh of relief. At last, I had Mommy. I had created a visual, kinesthetic experience of "Mother" for myself, a place I could go to, a womb I could curl up in. It was warm and dark and safe and silent.

Recently, I came across a poem I wrote about an all-red painting I did after my father died in 1979. It was four feet high by ten feet wide, on raw silk. I called it *Red*. Without knowing it, I had painted a Red Room. I include the poem here.

Red

I am
Graven pigeon
Task accomplished
A side of maximum efficiency
To a main of disorder.

All I ask for is a white wall
And RED inside of that
To rove in.

A simple order,
Immediate,
Spontaneous,
Exacting.

A poetic refrain,
A silent listener,
A tantric presence,
An absorbent
Endless
Empty
Rich
Field of Mind.

A place to go to,
Into,
Out of,
Because of.

I realized that with each of the deaths of my parents, I sought this same red room, this red space, which I believe to be the womb, whether physical or metaphysical, but how could I make this for myself, always? What was I looking for?

Once I had the Red Room—the Mother—I began to notice over a series of days that I was berating myself, calling myself names, ridiculing and shaming myself, in different places in my life. I found myself hating the Red Room, rejecting it, being angry with it, afraid of it, just as a child I had felt angry at and rejected by my mother. I realized I was living out loud an introjection[G] of my critical mother, which I had hidden and never owned in myself.

I was angry at myself because I wanted to write this book but, in my grief, I was living completely in a realm shared between my hurting inner child and my critical mother introject, and I didn't know if I was ever going to get out of that place so that I could write again.

I couldn't feel the masters around me although I knew, of course, that they were here. I couldn't even feel Yeshu and I felt I had abandoned and been abandoned by him. Magdalen I could feel faintly, when I called to her in my anguish and my confusion about where the I-who-I-had-known had gone, but even she was only a glimmer, because I was so disconnected from that "I" that I knew.

And then it came to me: somehow, now that my birth mother was truly dead, it was as if I had been set free to choose to keep the critical mother introject, or create instead a loving mother within. (I don't know why my psyche needed to wait until she was dead, but I allow that this was so.)

It was then that I realized I had no idea what "Mother," or the beloved, or the divine feminine was. I felt as if a whole part of my consciousness was still asleep, as it has been in the collective consciousness of much of humanity on this planet.

At last, I could begin.

2

MOTHER DARKNESS

May 22, 2009

How do I mother myself in a loving and tender way? Again, I ask, how do I treat myself as a beloved? Because my psyche led me to create the Red Room, I start my search there. Again, I put on my jammies, I light candles, close the door, get into bed, and then I call on Magdalen to help me.

I ask her now, as I have asked myself before, *What is the divine feminine? What is this "Mother" whose presence I am beginning to feel?* I can feel the formlessness in my psyche as a reflection of the formlessness of the realm of the unknown, the sacred mysteries of the feminine. There is a deep living darkness here, and I know it is exactly where I am meant to be, for it is within this darkness where all is created.

Magdalen speaks through me. Her very presence is in the room with me, as I record her words that come through my voice onto a laptop. She speaks to me, as to all, dear readers and all humanity for whom this book is written.

Magdalen: *I am here, dear one. I am here. You have called me today to speak about the Mother, and the divine feminine.*

What I bring to you today first, sweet one, is my commendation of all that you have done to prepare for this moment: your time preparing for the dark, your time in knowing that the dark time is of such importance at this time on the planet. There are many who live in the bright world, the fast-paced world where often there is not time to sit in the dark inside, the realm of inner knowing. There is then a disconnection from the self.

You have asked me to speak about the divine feminine, and it is this of which I speak today. It is a term, is it not, that is bandied about at this time now? Can anyone describe exactly what is this divine feminine? Can it be put into words at all? Or is it a place deep inside? A place in the wet, dark embryonic fluids of your being, at the depths of your soul?

You ask a large question, dear one, that the consciousness of the collective is asking now, without words, without even knowing, searching as if hungry to bring forth that which is already within.

 The collective unconscious knows the timeless silence, the unknown, the unnameable. This place is already embedded in all. In this place all are deeply held. Even now, dear one, feel yourself held. It is the feminine itself, the Mother, who holds you in this deepest realm of darkness.

You, dear one, have been driven to create this dark room, this cave. Allow this darkness, this unknown, this deepest mystery, to hold you, just as in the time of the womb, you were held physically. Allow that the divine feminine is the unknown itself, the mother darkness, a deep rich boundless love that comes from inside of you and all around you, always. There are no words for the boundless love that is here, as when the being has yet no words in the physical womb. There is a timelessness here. There are only sensations like dreams, and the knowing of being held by Source itself.

There is no "I" or ego or questions or thoughts or words, or content that involves language or space or time, past or future, or even physical body. There is no sense of time other than that of being held in the arms of an eternal now. Even the physicality of emotions is not found here, for there are no emotions yet.

It is a place of resting so deeply, laying your head down, your shoulders truly relaxed, the breath going out in absolute surrender, like a small child with her head on divine mother's lap. You, beloved, are finding this place in this moment with me now.

I in my incarnation as Mary Magdalen did not know this place until the time when I was twelve years of age. I was kept in my room, shunned by my family and village, sobbing in deep agony with the abandonment and loneliness I felt, until one morning, very early.

I had been in anguish many hours of the night, not knowing how I would survive a lifetime of being shunned—no touch, no talk, no healing contact—even from my mother. I was tired and desolate. I had given up, and I lay on my pallet in my room in the dark.

I looked out of the window and saw the morning star which had just arisen over the horizon. I curled myself, up tucking my feet under my robes, and I watched it rising slowly, higher and higher into the sky. Somehow, I felt different. I began to feel the darkness as love. It was a feeling of being held, not caring where my life would lead, not needing to know, just knowing that I was held in that darkness.

I feel right now, here in that place as I remember it, that I could sleep for days, in telling this. There is such calm. There is the calm of the infant being held in an eternal loving mother's arms, in such a place of trust that she can let herself sleep now. Let yourself feel this too now, and know that I am here with you always.

This is the Mother always with and within you.

I feel myself so sleepy now, and I can feel Magdalen, still faintly here, her energy surrounding me in this lull of peace. I feel held, in the dark, moist womb of the Mother.

I hear, *From the Mother comes all things, the darkness before light*. I think of cave paintings and sweat lodges. If Light is all things, then the dark is the absence of all things, the reassuring void. There are no expectations, or attachments, in the void of darkness. There is only silence, immeasurable, beyond words. There is a sense of safety. I feel myself resting in this place and being rocked to sleep.

Magdalen, I whisper, *I can feel the divine feminine, which lies beneath the ground, in the caves and hollows. Somehow, I too can feel the mother darkness lying deep inside me now. Is it truly already here within me and I just have to find the Mother within and learn her ways?*

Yes, dear one, whispers Magdalen. *Yes, dear one. She has always been a part of you, inside of you, that part that loves you deeply already.*

Thank you, I whisper. *Thank you.*

I have capitalized "Mother" because, for me, she is a facet of Source itself. I have not capitalized "the mother darkness" or "the divine feminine" because both come from a deep dark hidden place belonging to the feminine, and because it feels right to me that way.

I have also not capitalized "the loving mother within" because she is a place deep inside of me. There is an intimacy here for me with all of these terms and yet I capitalize "Mother" because she feels more like an archetype, a deity outside of me. I ask my readers to capitalize these terms or not, as they see fit. I do this in alignment with what feels right for me inside.

3

I, MAGDALEN

June 30, 2009

I can feel something happening deep inside me, an unfolding in the dark of my psyche, and all I can do is allow it and continue this path that I have begun. Again, I turn to Magdalen, sensing that the path leads through her to where I am meant to go next. I trust this because I trust her.

I ask her, *Magdalen, where do we go from here?*

I hear, *Begin at the beginning. Tell my story. Begin at my birth and allow me to tell it!*

It is as if I am a small child again, and this time I have a mother who tells me a story, and through the story, I learn who I am.

She continues, *I was treasured as the only child, even as a girl. Girls were of less import then, separated and excluded from many things in the Temple.*

Magdalen begins: *I come today, dear ones, as the Magdalene energy, speaking for the divine feminine, the Hidden Source, divine consort. I have been known by many names: Aphrodite, Diana, Hecate, Ishtar, Inanna, Holy Mother Mary, the goddess, the priestess, the whore, the virgin, the magician.*

I was not always beloved. There were long years when I lived as an outcast, a nonentity, shunned because of something I had unwittingly done as a young girl in my innocence. I paid for it a hundredfold and yet it gave me the wisdom and the wealth of love in that lifetime that I can now bring to you, dear ones.

I sit here with the masters, as so many have called us. We are facets of the Source of all light, all darkness, all that is known and all that is unknown. We are teaching energies. To name us, to label us, is to find a way to place us in your understanding. Perhaps you identify with some of us more than others, dear ones, and that is as it should be. Allow us to support you on your paths.

The channel's heart opens, glows with love. There is great delight in our love of her. For just as we chose to have me incarnate as Magdalen in that lifetime with Yeshu, my sweet Yeshu, as many call Jesus, so we have chosen to bring this one, the channel, into embodiment so that she may do this work for us.

There is so much love here. Her tears are our tears of joy, for we no longer have bodies that can feel the physical sensation of joy.

Together, we have chosen today to speak of how I came into that lifetime as Magdalen, for it was as an embodiment of the divine feminine that I came. And so we begin.

It seems as if from a dream, a time long ago, that I lived and breathed and loved in the body of Magdalen, the beloved of Yeshu.

We had already made the decision to send Yeshu, in body, to the planet. I came as Magdalen so that I could walk as the divine consort of Yeshu, the christed one, he who embodied the Great Love which is Source. As the divine consort, I would be his feminine counterpart— his love, his companion, his bedmate, his left hand, his support, his mother, his child, his beloved.

(Many and many have wondered, what do we the masters look like? The channel is wondering this now. We are crystalline forms of light. We can appear as humans or animals, or other beings, for we are shape-shifters. We can appear as anything of your imagination. We can appear as mother, father, sister, brother, tree, stone, flower, stream, the wind, god, goddess, darkness, or light. We are here to teach, love, support, guide, honor, cherish, and hold dear, you, our beloveds. In all ways, we are here, for you.)

When it came time for me to embody in that lifetime with Yeshu, I remember forming myself, slowing down my frequencies, honing to the earth plane. I remember calling myself to those who became the seed and the egg that formed me. I found a man to be the father. He was an older man in his sixties. I found with him a wife who was quiet and loving, for that was what I chose for myself for that lifetime, to imprint into that embodiment.

Here where I sit in the masters' hall, I remember the time in the womb. I remember all of this. I remember the warmth there, the throbbing of the blood, the pulse of the heartbeat, knowing it as I knew the moon, the tides, the planets, the universes. As the time for me to appear came closer, I remember the feeling of not enough room! Tight, being bound in that womb! And wanting to be set free into this new experience that was human life. I had experienced human life before, the "I" that was the emanation of the divine feminine, but I allowed myself to forget, before I was born, so that this experience could be new.

The entire time in that womb, I felt the love and tenderness of that mother, who had been in despair that she was barren, and who was so full of joy and wonderment that she would at last bear a child—her husband hoping it would be a son, and her secretly hoping it would be a daughter to give her the companionship that she had always wished for.

I was born squalling, of course, not understanding this light bright world! And I was quickly washed and anointed and brought to my mother's arms for her to view me. My father came. He was somewhat disappointed because I was a girl, but very glad for his wife because he loved her. And there was a certain tenderness in his eyes as he beheld me then and many times after.

I was not fed at my mother's breast but instead was given to a young slave named Martha who had birthed a child who had died. It was at her breast that I began to remember who I was, for she had no shame about her body, the way many had at that time. She taught me to be free in my body.

And so I grew. I reveled in playing, as little girls will. Martha took me to the shore where I played naked in the sand. I loved the feel of the sand on my body. I would roll in the sand, and then run laughing into the lapping waves. I had no fear of the water, for did I not come from the water? Was the water not in a way my Mother?

I delighted in the shells! I would bring a shell to my ear and listen and squeal with delight at the sounds of the sea; and I would bring the shell to my room, from that beautiful Sea of Galilee.

I was left alone for much of the time, for Martha had other duties. I was left to wander in the courtyards of our white stone house. There were many courtyards in our house, many servants, for my father was a rich merchant. I had silks and perfumes and mirrors from the Far East, and beautiful clothes. My room was draped with fabrics of many colors and many textures.

I reveled in the feelings of them. I would let them slide along my naked body. I loved to touch my skin. Even as a little girl, I loved to smooth the creams and oils on my legs and face and arms, on my breasts that were not breasts yet, but merely small buds. Sometimes, my mother would come in to see what I was doing, not often, for she was somewhat poorly after my birth. And she would stop me and shame me and say, No, this is not seemly! What you are doing is not seemly!

And I would run to her crying and apologize, wrapping my arms around her waist, and I would look up into her eyes, my eyes streaming with tears. I would say, Mama, I am sorry, please forgive me. I do not understand. Will you please tell me, what is wrong with my body? What is wrong with being naked? What is wrong, please, with loving the feelings here, the textures of this cloth? I do not understand. What is wrong with these feelings?

She would look at me in silence. I could see the compassion in her eyes, the love flowing from her heart, her gentle hands stroking my hair. She would put her finger to her lips and say, Shhhh. We may not speak of this, dear one. It is forbidden. It is the law.

So I grew up not understanding, knowing that in the outside world there was something wrong, something shameful about the female body. We never spoke of the male body, of course! I never thought to speak of it, or to ask of it!

I only knew of my body. And I assumed that there was merely, and exclusively, a law written which made the female body taboo. But in my room, and inside, in the hidden places of my being, I knew that there was nothing wrong. I knew that my body was a beloved part of myself.

How could I shun that which I was? Was that not denying my self? How could I separate myself from my legs, my arms, my heart, my secret places, my belly, my feet, my face? My neck that carries this head? My hair that grows and curls so beautifully? My eyes that look out at myself in the hand mirror that I hold, my eyes which speak volumes to me of my heart and soul? How could I shun that which I am? I learned to keep this knowing secret.

I still went to the shore. I picked up rocks and shells and studied them and saw the body of them in wonderment. As I saw my own body in wonderment. As I saw the flowers in wonderment. As I saw the sea in wonderment, and the buildings, and all things, all forms, all shapes, all colors, all hues. For were not these all sacred and beautiful and merely what they were, as they embodied the soul of what they were?

I had two boy cousins who would visit with their families on feast days. At times, we would visit their homes and share Sabbath with them. These two boy cousins, Jacob and Samuel, were born around the time that I was born, and we grew up together, as infants and small children. We played on the shore together.

The slaves who were bought for them came with Martha and me, bringing us to the shore so that they could laugh and gossip and tell stories to each other, as we played on the shore harmlessly. I would show the boys the shells, and we would rub our cheeks together. I would lay my small hand on the cheek of Jacob or Samuel, and look right into his eyes, and say, Look at what I have found! Isn't it beautiful?

In those times, when we were small, there was an answering warmth, and an agreement, an answering wonderment. And we strode arm in arm, our arms around each other's waists. We would giggle and wrestle and laugh, and play in the waves together, and fling water at each other, tumbling in the waves and gathering sand on our bodies, and tumble and gather sand on our bodies again, sometimes naked but for a loincloth for the boys, later. When we were very small, we ran naked! There was no one to say no in those early days.

But then, as we grew, the wrestling began to change. The boys began to learn from their fathers the prowess of what it was to be a man. They began to see a supremacy of man over woman, and they punched me and berated me for being a mere girl.

They began to give me strange looks when I would touch my body or touch theirs, innocently. Not in their private places! No, surely! I would take a shell and rub it down an arm, innocently, and say, Feel this! Feel this! And then I'd laugh joyously and run into the water!

There came a haunted look in their eyes, a look of fear and torn confusion. They did not understand that which was inside of themselves, which was inside me, my owning and accepting and loving of my body. They could not place that with what they were taught.

There came a day when I was twelve years of age and I went to the shore, still with Martha. Still I skipped but now in gowns, my headscarf hiding my hair, as was the custom, but still finding the shells, my gown pulled up a little, to step into the water.

I began to hear on the shore behind me the muted sound of many feet and, as I looked, I saw Jacob and Samuel leading a group of boys. They rushed upon me and threw me down and called me names and pummeled me, in my private places and my breasts. They tore my clothes, pulled off my robes, and called me "whore," because they did not understand this love I had for my body.

They scratched at my face and kicked me and threw me into the waves, and then they dragged me up along the rocks and shells which scored my body and tore my skin and my clothes.

I cried out, not understanding. I looked directly into Samuel's face, into Jacob's face, and I said, Why? Why are you doing this?

And there was a gruff response: Because you are a whore. It is known. You shame us in knowing you. We do not own you as our cousin. We shun you.

One of them took a rock and hit me hard on the head, and there was blackness and silence after that.

The next thing I can remember, I was lying on my pallet at home, in the dark, alone and in great pain, at first not remembering. And then, like a great wave, the grief, the pain of my beloved cousins turning against me washed over me. This pain was much greater than the pain of my body. For I knew, from somewhere deep inside of me, that this was the shunning of the feminine. I was shunned for loving myself. There was much in the Temple that was called sacred but, to me, this was the shunning of the most sacred, for if we cannot love ourselves, how then can we love at all?

I had not understood this before. With this understanding came an even greater sadness, a great grief in my heart that more than matched the pain between my legs where the boys had grabbed me and beaten me and pretended to have conquest of me.

I did not know that I was beautiful. I merely saw myself as a dreamer girl, often scolded by my mother for being forgetful. I did not know that the boys of my age and older were mesmerized by my beauty, drawn to the inexplicable feminine energy which I exuded without realizing.

From that day forward, I was shunned by my cousins and their friends. I was shunned by my mother and my father, and the people of the village of Magda, for all believed that I was a fallen woman, a prostitute, a whore. My cousins, in their fear, had named me so. People ceased to touch me. I was spoken to by no one. I was treated as if I were worse than dead.

My bright youthful garments were put away and I was given only grey to wear, grey robes, a grey headdress, for the message was that I was a ghost. It was as if I did not exist in the eyes of the family and the village.

For a time, I wept bitterly and then I began to take hold of myself, mastered my resolve. I did not weep again, not for a long time. I closed my heart to those around me and lived as a stone figure. Slowly, I learned to bury that part of myself that had been alive, and to look at and speak to and touch no one.

At first, the pain was unbearable. I would not have survived if it had not been for Martha who would speak to me in whispers, in private only. It was she who gently put the salves on my bruises and cuts. It was she who, little by little, smuggled in a mirror and other things, so that I could see that I was indeed healing. She was forbidden to come in for more than a moment at a time, other than to tend my wounds and bring me food, and I was forbidden to leave my room.

I had many dreams during that time, often of a dark, hidden place that held me in safety. During that time I was very feverish. I do not know if someone came to tend to me or if I was left undisturbed. But when I came out of that fever, I had come to a peace inside of myself, an acceptance of the knowledge that I was shunned.

It was at that time that my inner world began to grow. I began to speak inside to my body that was the temple of my soul, and I let it know that I still loved it, that it was still a Holy of Holies to me. I did not completely know my purpose or the path that I would take, but I was not afraid. Within myself, I grew strong.

Because the room had only a small window, I would light the oil lamps to have the company of their fire, for in their flames I knew *there was life force. It mirrored the life force of my heart, and of my soul. The silence of the flames mirrored the silence within me that was so profound and full.*

I knew that there was for me a life beyond this one.

Even though I was shunned and treated as a ghost, gradually, over time, I was allowed to leave my room. My mother still did not speak to me, or look at or touch me, but I knew that she felt a great sadness that she no longer had a daughter as companion. She would not see me marry, nor would she hold her grandchildren. I would not join her with the other women, in the rituals at the Temple. She grew weaker, and there was nothing I could do.

I was allowed to go to the well to fetch water on the feast days when the servants were busy, when it was hoped that most of the people of Magda were either in the temple or in their homes. It was a great freedom to me, even though I dreaded it at the same time, for I knew I would be shunned at the well, and ridiculed and perhaps stoned, if anyone saw me.

Even in painful times, there are great gifts given. On an especially cruel day, I went to the well, thinking that few would be about. Just as I was filling my urn, there came, purposefully, spitefully, the mother of one of the boys who had attacked me, knowing I might be alone. She pushed me down, and the urn broke and lost all its water. As she was throwing stones at me, and calling me names, it was at that moment that the magic began. It came unbidden, in the form of a golden voice, which said, not in words but inside me, Behold the light within. Behold the light around you, that you are.

In that moment, I began to see things differently, the light of things. I began to listen to the things of nature, to what they were saying and what they might teach me. I began to hear the voices of the angels, the faeries, and the invisibles around me. I began to have a sense of belonging, much greater than ever before, a belonging to a place rooted deep inside that was part of a greater universe, of nature and the planets and all beings. I did not name it so then, but I felt secure in the knowledge of my place in all things, within me.

As I grew older, a sense of expectancy grew. I began to dream of someone of great import appearing before me as from beyond a veil. The magic grew within me, too. It peopled the world for me, with the light and auras of the invisibles, and I was further shunned for the way in which I would look at things that for others were not there. I would speak to beings that others did not see. It was said that I spoke in tongues, that I harnessed demons to me, that I was a witch in those times. What I saw was the etherics^G of all things, and what I heard was the etherics of their voices.

One day, when I was seventeen years of age, I covered my face and hair with my grey scarf, as was the custom before going out. I placed the empty urn on my head. I walked to the well slowly, trying to attract as little attention as possible, balancing the urn, holding my hips in such a way that they did not sway, holding in that of me which was my natural self, which I know now is sacred, and making myself grey, blank, nameless, as bodiless as possible.

I set my urn down and shut my ears to the ridicule, to the name-calling and spiteful laughter, the stones that fell around my feet and grazed my shoulder and back, for there were a few women there after all. I sat on the well's edge and reached for the pail to send it down the well, to fill my urn. And then, I heard a man's voice. Will you give me water, he said. I have great thirst.

I closed my eyes and grimaced with the pain of it. I tried to close my heart, weeping inside with the pain of being spoken to, after so many years. And yet in this voice, I heard such great love. In this voice, I heard no judgment.

I froze. I swallowed.

I took a deep breath and closed my eyes more tightly, wincing, so afraid was I of the scorn I might receive if I were to respond to this man who had spoken to me. I took another deep breath, and I mustered my courage. I opened my eyes, not daring to look at him. I pulled up the pail, and I reached for the ladle and filled it. I set down the pail, and I knelt, as I must, as a woman, as this woman, this ghost.

I held the ladle towards him, my eyes still cast down and, as I did so, he touched me. He took my arm, and he said, Come. Stand. There is no need to kneel before me.

My heart cried out, for again there was gentleness in his voice as he spoke to me. He had touched me, as no one had done for so long, and he held my arm to help me stand.

In that moment, I looked into his eyes and I saw... I saw my beloved! I saw as if I were seeing the hidden part of myself in his eyes! I saw the sacred in his eyes. I saw the love in his eyes. He was the embodiment of a Great Love, Source itself, even though at that time I had no name for it.

I weep now in the telling, as the channel weeps with me.

It was as if he really saw me. He looked into my eyes. He looked into my heart. He looked into the center of me. I was no longer alone. I was washed by a light. Oh dear ones, the channel has tears, my tears, on her cheeks, as I tell this. Oh, dear ones, as I remember that moment, as I looked into his eyes, I looked into his soul also, and I knew him.

In that moment, there was something like an echo, a whisper, a memory of recognition from long ago. I can tell you now that it was our two souls remembering, but as a young woman, in body, I did not know that. I only knew the feeling of it.

As I put the ladle to his mouth, his hand cupping mine, a stream of lights moved through me from that touch. I looked into his eyes and his looked into mine—heart to heart, soul to soul—and I knew that here was my path. Here was my life. Here was my soul. Here was my future, my past, my destiny. Here was all that I was, all that I am. And I was washed in the peace of that moment.

All grief left me. All pain left me. I heard not the others around us, for it was as if we were in a halo that included only the two of us in its great light. Together we were complete. He said to me, Will you come with me? Will you teach and guide me? Will you follow me and let me show you the way? Will you join with me?

And I said, yes, and that was the beginning. That was the beginning of my path with my dear beloved. And I know, dear ones, that I would not have known him, truly, if I had not experienced all that went before.

It was many years later that I learned that the boys that day on the lake had only lain on top of me and torn my clothes and beaten me out of their frustration and their fear of who and what I was. It was not until the first time I lay with Yeshu and I bled, that I knew that I was still a virgin, and untouched.

The harm was done, however, and the village believed what it believed. For those beliefs I am deeply grateful, for it was my solitude that awakened the magic within me.

I thank this one for asking, "Where shall we begin?" I thank this one, my beloved channel, and the masters around me.

I thank Source for giving me the great gift of remembrance in this body of the channel here, of that time then, of that meeting with my beloved Yeshu and all that went before. And I ask that those who hear these words know now what it is to hold the self sacred, to hold the body sacred, as the divine consort to Source itself, as I was to my dear Yeshu, in body and soul.

Thank you for this channeling, beloved channel.

I leave you now, in love and in joy.

4

AFTER MAGDALEN

June 30, 2009

Coming back from long ago, as it was, I whisper, *Thank you,* a trace of tears still on my face. Tears of grief for the little girl that I was who did not feel safe in her body, as the young Magdalen did. Tears of longing and hope for Magdalen as she was seen at last by Yeshu and pulled gently, lovingly, out of her isolation. Too, tears of joy and gratitude at the gift of sharing such a thing as Magdalen's experience as she tells her story.

What would it have been like, I wonder now, to have grown up innocent, pure, safe in my body, instead of having that unsettling, unnameable feeling that there was always something wrong with me, something for which I felt shame? For a long time, I didn't know what that was or where it came from. I didn't know how much I was out of body, as a child, living in the faery tales I read to escape the feelings of being lost, bewildered, and not knowing why, not even wondering why, just assuming that that was how it is to be a child growing up. How would I have known what was normal, if there was such a thing? All I knew was that I was flawed somehow.

Maybe that's why I loved nature so much, and still do, because that is where I can have the sensate experiences of wind and water on my skin, earth beneath my feet, flower scents and faery chimes. Maybe nature has been a place where I can be in body safely, owning it and appreciating being human.

I hear, *Yes, that's right, dear one, as I did.*

As Magdalen's story came through me, it was not as if I were re-living that early time, as a young girl, free, whole, playfully and lovingly connected with my body and myself, but as if I was living it for the first time.

How can I explain this? This feeling I had through Magdalen, of knowing at my core that I am grounded in myself, safe inside of my own body. Is this what it is to have the Mother, the divine feminine, this inner knowing of who I am, firmly rooted inside?

I know now, as I write this, that just as Yeshu embraced Magdalen with that great love of Source, she gave back to him a firmly rooted inner strength of self, that became his rock.

Yes, dear one. I was his rock, his tower, and he was my great love. Nothing could shake that place inside of me that came in that time of isolation. When Yeshu found himself in despair of getting his mes-

sage across, he would seek me out, just to look into my eyes, so that he might see and be reminded of that deep inner strength of the feminine, and he was restored.

This is what we want for you, dear ones. We want you to know that place inside. We offer our love and support, as you each walk the path of finding it for yourself.

I think I am beginning to understand now that, just as Yeshu was an embodiment of the great love of Source, so the divine feminine instills a deep hidden well of love within us, for ourselves. It is as if by loving myself from that place, Source's love comes from inside of me, like a mirror of that love all around me. *Magdalen, is it this that gave you a sense of belonging? Is that what you mean by the divine consort?*

Magdalen responds: *Yes, dear one. You do understand. For when you love yourself, you are as Source loving you. Yeshu showed us how Source is a great love, and that all beings are loved. Now, it is for humanity to learn to love itself, with that same love of Source, from a place deep within.*

Dear ones, all readers, allow my spoken words to activate deep within you, so that you may know of what I speak, that I was beloved, that I belonged to a greater world of Beloveds, as one of the all, and what it is to be held in that knowledge.

Know that you too are beloved, dear ones, as is all humanity. We delight in the dawning of this new age of the divine feminine, that comes from within. How we love your thirst to learn this, dear channel—and all others who thirst.

Thank you again, Magdalen, I say. *Thank you. That is what I feel sometimes inside me too, but I so easily lose it.*

I wonder, can the invisible inside be destroyed? I don't think so and yet I feel that happening so often when I lose my power.

5

THE FLAME OF CREATION

July 6, 2009

I am still thinking about all that Magdalen said a few days ago. I am especially struck by how she seemed to belong to the world of light—Source's world all around her—and yet when she met the man Yeshu, the pain of her isolation was still so strong that she winced at the possibility that he too might reject her.

For years, I have loved being alone, writing, walking, talking to myself around the house, creating; yet there are instances when I feel separate, different, even lonely, and have wished that I really belonged to the world of people, not just the light. I have friends and people who love me in my life, but somehow I have still felt at times that I don't belong, really belong, in three-dimensional form anywhere on this planet.

Even when I find a beautiful place to walk, like along the Pacific Ocean on the wild lone beaches of Moss Landing and Big Sur, walking the coastline or the high open plains of the British Isles, my heart feels a deep sorrow of separation.

I know that my soul's lineage began, long ago, when Source in a moment of divine inspiration, split itself into a myriad of sparks—called monads^G—and each of our souls is descended from one of those original sparks. I have often wondered at both my easy sense of belonging to the light, as well as this other feeling of isolation and separation.

I believe that part of being on the path of the beloved, searching for and finding myself as a beloved, is knowing where I came from, affirming that I came in as part of Source itself. In this moment, I want to explore what it felt like, what my experience was then, at my beginning, and so I move into the place of the channel now to go back to that time.

As channel, I close my eyes and allow myself to go spiraling back to that time, and already I can feel myself there as I tell it. I can feel the expansion of joy in my etheric heart, as Source. I can feel the excitement, the anticipation, the expectancy, and the boundless love in knowing that in this creation moment, as Source, I expand myself, multiplying into a myriad of individual, creative beings who have all of the facets and possibilities of the glory that I am.

I can feel also the grief, knowing of the shadow that I as Source create and, therefore, that all sparks, all individual souls, will be traversing before returning again to my fold, as Source.

The grief itself is not around any judgment of mine as Source around the shadow but simply my knowledge that I must not interfere, even though I live through each and every experience, as each and every spark lives it.

Bringing myself back to here and now, I think that my sense of belonging, as well as my feelings of isolation and separation, are wrapped up in that first moment of my sparking, and I want to know more, so again I call on Magdalen. This time, I feel as if I am allowing myself to merge with her, or maybe it is my own higher consciousness that is coming through, as I listen with my etheric ears and all of my being.

Magdalen and the channel as one: *I am remembering the time when I began, the moment of my first sparking. I am immersed in the place before the light of Source.*

Source itself is the mother darkness, in a time before time. I as Source am the boundless desire to love, the boundless energy of love. I am profound darkness and I rest in this place, in myself as Source, in myself as this darkness. I am yet not awakened and yet I can feel the resting, almost as a lullaby. There is a deep cradling of the being that I am at this time and yet am not. For I am consciousness and yet I am not yet conscious of myself.

I am surrounded by a deep maternal darkness. It is a place of safety, deep love, mystery, a fathomless unknown. I am complete within myself. There is about me no desire, no wish, no want. It is a time without time, of the gestation of Source itself.

This time-without-time lasts, endures, through an eternity.

There comes a time in this gestation when this mother darkness, this Source that I am, begins to notice, without conscious awareness of self, a subtle urge to create that which can reflect me, that which can converse with and expand me—that which can mirror and feed, sustain, embellish, and create me, as if creation creates itself.

And this too takes an eternity in the linear time of humanity, and yet happens as if in the blink of an eye.

How can I describe the profound excitement, the exquisite delight, the love beyond joy in the moment when Source comes to the idea to create the pinpoints of light that we are?

Allow yourselves, dear ones, and I speak now to all, as the channel and Magdalen, along with many masters. Allow yourselves to sink into this experience of being Source itself, the mother darkness itself, that profound, loving, sweet, tangible, silent, boundless darkness of the unknown that is the Mother, that is Source.

And then suddenly, with an incomparable brilliance, she/he/it creates the splinters, the points of light, the sparks that become each of us now present in our bodies! The Divine Arc Welder arcing out its flame of creation!

I who in this moment am Source, all creation, as well as the channel herself, wish for you, beloved readers, to imagine this brilliance, this moment, this flash of lights—from all points of Source! I wish you to imagine that you have, in your hand, a remote control that slows this moment down, lengthens out this brilliant moment so that you can step into, and inside of, and be, this flame itself, this Flame of Creation.

Allow yourselves now to be Source, as mother darkness, in her profound love, gifting her creations (those individual splinters of light) with the beauty of her experience. At the same time, allow yourselves to be the spark that you came from. Allow yourselves now to step into the brilliant warm deep red golden blue green yellow violet purple—all the colors of the flame of your creation.

Slow down in time so that you can feel, within that flame, Source's immense love, boundless joy, and delight in a connection that goes beyond eternity. Know in this moment, as I do, that not only is the concept of leaving Source, or separation from Source, a fallacy, but we are ourselves Source in the very moment of the flame of our creation!

Magdalen speaking now for the masters: *The picture that we see today is Source as a golden ball of light like the sun. The rays of this light are each one of you connecting, through the divine plan of your soul, to Source for eternity. The channel's heart fills with love, and joy beyond joy, at this image.*

I lay this before you, knowing what is true, that you are as much Source as Source itself. You are the rays, each and every one of you. You are the brilliance. You are every color in the rainbow of light that emanates from Source. You are the mother darkness even before the light began.

And we, the masters, who are here now with you, did we not come also from this Source? Are we not also rays of this brilliance?

Are we not also reflecting back to this immensity, this eternity, this beauty, this profound love that is Source? So how are we then masters above you?

I, Leslie, can feel the palms of my hands tingling, for I have unconsciously raised them into the air, face up, and I can feel the immense energy of the masters speaking through me, of Source's excitement and joy in this moment. I can feel the love of the masters, as emanations of Source moving through me, and it is profound.

There are so many, continue the masters, *who have felt abandoned, lonely, rejected and dejected, and have believed that they were separate from Source. When you have those feelings, allow yourselves to remember the extended moment of the Flame of Creation, remember that you are a ray of Source's light eternally imbued with that connection.*

Know this now, dear ones.

We have observed the etheric rivers of many souls tracing the karma^G of their lifetimes all the way back to that monadic moment that happened so quickly that there was a mistaken belief of separation from Source at that time.

Know now that that separation never happened!

There is a time between lifetimes for each soul that I call the "spark-of-light time," when we look at our previous lifetimes and plan the next one. I see this place as a big conference room with a big oval conference table and chairs, where we each meet with our own cosmic boards: soul groups, teachers, counselors, and players for the next lifetime.

Here the soul has access to the wisdom of the monad and Source, and decisions are made on how best to play out and clear the karma for the next lifetime. The souls of those who will people the lifetime are called to the table, to orchestrate and bring forth the greatest practice and learning so that all the souls involved can continue to advance.

I feel the ascended master Vywamus[G] coming in. One of his main functions is to assist in channeling. (I refer to Vywamus as male for ease of reference, even though he has never incarnated.) Here he acts as an ally to help me move through my own sense of separation for all time. I have this beautiful image now of the creation moment. He is saying, *It is very important that all souls remember the immersion moment in Source's Flame of Creation.*

I, as channel, can feel it now. *I am standing in a waterfall of sparks of every color. They are not hot like hot coals but rather hot with the magic of Source itself, as I am, in this moment. I am completely immersed in this shower of the Flame of Creation so that all time stops. I become this Flame of Creation. I allow this experience to embed and imprint into my eternal soul's being, my I-AM-ness, so that I may be free of the wounds of the fallacy that I was ever separate.*

Magdalen: *Imagine this waterfall made of sparkling creation dust, many-faceted sparkles with every color of the rainbow inside each particle, showering all around you; these are the energetic components of this Flame of Creation that connects you for all time to Source itself.*

Allow yourself now to be this Flame of Creation, this connection. Allow yourself to be Source itself, at the same time as you are your eternal individual soul. This is a moment of deep connection, in which you are the Source that creates you.

I ask you to feel this and allow this in every particle of your being—in every atom, molecule, cell, past-present-future-parallel lifetime, backwards and forwards to the divine plan of your soul, NOW! With the intention that this moment becomes a river of this moment, one that floods your ancient and archetypal lineage backwards and forwards to the beginning of time, to the divine plan itself, and Source itself, so that you are imbued with this experience!

Allow this moment to create a tingling in your hands, a tingling in your heart, as you place your hands on your heart, as your physical anchor, as you stand in this waterfall that is the Flame of the Creation of Source that is you, that is me.

Dear ones, whispers Magdalen, whisper the masters, *feel our love. Feel the love of Source now. Know that embedded within Source is the place where you belong, the Mother within.*

We offer this to you with all of our love, devotion, compassion, and desire to hold you and love you, in all moments, when you ask, or when your divine consciousness allows it.

Dear ones, we ask you to rest in the moment of the Flame of Creation. We ask you to linger here and return to this place often.

For you are beloved of us.

You are beloved of the divine mystery that is Source, that is the Mother.

You are beloved, dear ones. Always loved, always held, always cherished, always seen, always heard, always known.

Always known.

Rest in this, beloveds. Rest in this.

And know that when you call, we are with you.

In the name of the light that you are.

I thank Magdalen and all who assisted, for the beautiful words and images that came today. I truly feel that I can rest in this place of belonging now, as Source, as spark, as soul.

And yet, I also know that the original monadic wound of separation and the fears that come with it feel very real to many of us, as they did for Magdalen when she met Yeshu at the well. I believe that the more I allow myself to bask in the truth of my Sourceness, in that uninterrupted love, the more I will be able to see those fears, when they come up, as merely a layer of them releasing for all time.

I thank all that came today for the insights and energies and truths imparted. It was a welcome and timely embrace.

6

THE HIDDEN SOURCE

July 17, 2009

I am in two places. One is the place of self-doubt and confusion about my abilities to channel a clear explanation of the divine feminine, about which I know so little.

The other place is where I live in my soul, and it brings me to this chapter. Somehow, I know that in the deepest darkest etheric caverns of the universes, as in ourselves, magic lies waiting like a sleeping dragon. These caverns are the realm of the Hidden Source, the divine feminine, bound in silence and mystery, older than time and older than Source as we know it.

This morning when I was asking Magdalen about the divine feminine, as we prepared for this channeling, she said: *It is that deep unconscious place of the mother darkness before Source created itself into splinters of light.*

I now call forth the energies of the divine feminine, so that that which has been hidden may be revealed.

I call forth Magdalen in her most beautiful presence, as ambassador to humanity, ushering forth the divine feminine into conscious state on this planet, as all planets.

I call forth sweet Yeshu to support us in this endeavor. I call forth Buddha who also represents the feminine. I call forth those of light, those masters, angels, devas[G]—dear nature spirits of the plants—and the faeries of light, and all who are meant to join with us today in this channeling.

I call forth the pure white crystalline light of the highest healing order. I ask to be surrounded in a sphere of this light. I ask to be re-created into a perfected crystalline form, so that I may transmit the channeling with clarity, compassion, love, and wisdom.

And I thank all of those who are here in this moment, for what comes today. Thank you in the name of the light.

I ask Magdalen, *How did the divine feminine—the power of the feminine, the magic of the feminine—how did it get buried, and why?*

She comes in now.

Magdalen: Dear one, dear one (laughing)! You ask how the divine feminine got buried and why?

And I answer, Why not?

And you and many—there are so many—who ask, What is the divine feminine?

Allow yourself to remember the place of that profound unknown, of the darkness before Source re-created itself into splinters of light so that it would be known, so that it would know itself.

Here is the answer in its simplicity.

The mother darkness, the divine feminine, that which is the unknown—the unknowable, the unnameable—has remained hidden, the hidden part of Source itself, because it had not the desire to know itself.

It is the realm of the unknown that lies hidden in your dreams, in your wishes, in the breeze that goes by and ruffles your hair. It is the silent deep urgings of your psyche.

How to make this known.

It is not until now that the collective consciousness truly wants to recognize and own the unknown within itself, within its unconscious. It is true that there have been matriarchal societies at various times across the planet but we are not speaking of gender, are we? We are speaking of the divine feminine itself, the qualities and attributes of that which comes from Source. Hence, the exploration.

Dear one, we have always been with you. When I say "you," I speak to all readers, all peoples, all beings, all planets, all universes.

Yes, the sleeping dragon awakes. We have said this, have we not? But it is not a waking that is defined as the waking that you know. It is a different sort of waking.

It is looking into the darkness and knowing, simply, that it is the unknown and the unnameable, and allowing that that is so. It is allowing the unnameable to have room in a realm of the known and the named, and the labeled, and the boxed, and the sorted.

The channel read my words in the Nag Hammadi Library,[5] before this channeling began, because her own unconscious has been driven to find these answers, and knew that she must. What is written there is that Mary—that incarnation that I was, Mary Magdalen— spoke to the apostles and said, Let that which is hidden be revealed.[6]

We speak to all and to many. We know that our words are translated into the energies and languages of all of those who listen and connect with this channeling today, to the entire planet and all planets, to make conscious that which has been unconscious.

To say that the hidden is to be revealed is to then understand that you will not be looking with your eyes, or hearing with your ears, or feeling with your hands or skin, or the physicality of your body.

No. For it is the hidden in you—your inner sense, your inner knowing, without thoughts, without words, without content—that will see, hear, sense, and understand the hidden of the divine feminine. It is an entirely different language of revealing.

The planet is ready for this now.

The collective consciousness is ready for this to come forth now.

Why do you think that the United States Post Office has put out stamps of the King and Queen of Hearts, at this time now, in 2009? (Magdalen is laughing.)

Perhaps you do not understand this cosmic joke.

The King, or the masculine, the Source of all love and light that wanted to know itself, to know more, to experience itself *through all of those monadic^G splinters of light! That is one side of the coin!*

The flip side, if you will, is the Queen, the feminine, who has no desire to know herself, who feels absolutely safe, complete, whole, in her identity as the unknown, the unknowable, the unnamed, the unnameable.

We humans try to name everything, do we not, so that we can understand? And I speak as "we humans" for I remember the times when I lived in human body, and I allow myself to be with you here, as human and also as ascended master—as one—in these channelings, to more fully experience what you experience, dear ones, so that I may help you to understand.

Yes, this need to name everything is the masculine side of us. This is the part of us that came directly from Source, wishing to know itself more.

And now, at last, dear ones, comes the richness, and I do not say that Source is not rich! Ah! How could I say such a thing? Source is rich beyond measure. Source is boundless beyond measure. I dearly love Source. I dearly love all that is known. I dearly love all that is named.

And I also love—with a love that is unnameable, that lies deep beneath the consciousness of its loving—the unknown, the unknowable, the unnamed, the unnameable.

And yes, I say this many and many times, because each time I say it, it begins a stirring, an activation, an initiation. And those who listen, in the energies around us that transmit to the planet, to all beings, to all planets, to all universes—they know that this does occur.

There was a great mystery to what it was to be woman, to the blood time, which long ago, and in some primitive peoples still today, came with the tide, the moon, the pulse of the earth. Women gathered in the bleeding huts, the bleeding tents during their blood time, to be separated from the men, to be in the mystery and because men feared the power of this mystery.

That mysterious pulse is part of that which is unnameable. It is the pulse inside each and every being now, that begins to stir.

We are trying to put words to that which has no words.

It is time on this planet for humanity to embrace that which is unknown within itself, that which is the unnameable within itself. For in this unnameable place, lying within this Hidden Source, if you will, is the magic that brews all creation.

How do we define magic? Shall we try to define the indefinable? For how can we explain that the word "magic" itself evokes a feeling of magic?

The magic of dreams. The magic of an idea in the imagination.

The inexplicable feeling—a tingling, a shivering or some other sign—that comes when you feel, in your entire being, the thrill of the presence of something outside of yourself, unseen and unheard, and knowing from a place hidden deep inside, that it is of the divine.

The doe, blanched by moonlight, crossing the snow-laden field, as she stops and sees you—your breath held, filled with awe at the sense of unreality—the magic of that one ethereal moment.

Looking into the eyes of another for the first time and knowing that you have known each other before, the inexplicable magnetic draw between you that makes your blood rush and your pulse rise, a draw that is made up of both of you and yet is more than the two of you combined.

The in-between-time between darkness and dawn when all the world lies sleeping and you are held in the breathtaking secret of your own potent invisibility.

Walking in the woods and knowing that the trees are alive and watching, and that they have always known and protected you, no matter what form you take now, since time began.

The tingling inside, the catch of your breath, the tears of rightness in your heart, that tell you that who you are in that moment is beyond the you that calls yourself "I."

The hush of grace, the presence of the divine, or Source, and knowing that you are a part of it, connected to it.

A moment of expectancy, the thrill of it held in a knowing inside that is unexplained and inexplicable.

There is no detailed description. There is only the knowing and the feeling of grace, being in the presence of that something-else that is beyond and yet of you. And it harbors within it a magic, a potential of creativity that says all things are possible. And yet the creativity itself and the term "all things are possible" live in the realm of Source, the Revealed Source, if you will, that which wanted to know itself.

What comes from the Hidden Source is the brewing and the magic of the potential from which all creation comes.

The initiate of Merlin and St. Germaine^G (ascended master of magic and transformation) *stands before a group of people raising her arms and breathing out a semblance of fire. She becomes in that moment a huge blue-black dragon—as she describes it to them, whispering—raising her wings and pulling from the ethers and the air all around, a stirring of the presence of that dragon in each and every one of her listeners so that they, in their minds' eyes and their etheric bodies, raise their wings and become as dragons too.*

The stirring that fills the room comes from the Hidden Source, from the time before Source became conscious of itself.

Imagine it in this moment, here, now.

The flower bulb raises its face to the moonlight and breaks the earth's surface in the hush of night. The silent observer feels the magic, yet who can explain it, describe it, replicate it?

The devas and faeries of the garden access the energy of the Hidden Source, the divine feminine, to perform their healing. The shamans, when they go deep into the earth, leading the journey, where they meet the root people, the rock people, the center of the earth people—they are tapping into this Hidden Source.

The masters around me are saying that the magic that spins from this Hidden Source, that derives from this place of the unnameable, the unknowable, the unknown, is one of fertility, fecundity, possibility, expectancy. To tap into it is to tap into the realm of all possibility that comes before manifestation and creation.

It is a hidden pull, a force that lies within the sleeping dragon deep in the cave of all beings. Deep, dark, unknown, hidden, and yet holding the immeasurable power of potential, of alchemy, of that which is beyond the self and yet encompasses the self.

When that which comes from the mother darkness, the Hidden Source, unfolds itself to be revealed, in that waking moment, the magic is felt and known and, thus, creates something beyond the self, bringing the self to the realm of Source. The dragon wakes, the kundalini^G flames spiral, and Source creates itself anew.

For a long time, humanity has avoided that which is hidden in itself and seen it as only shadow, something to fear. It has not understood that the greatest inventions, the most beautiful art, the most refined writings, the most angelic music, is revealed through making known that which originated within the Hidden Source, the divine feminine.

And once humanity—once the collective consciousness—allows this truth, then all that comes with that Hidden Source will also be accepted and embraced, applauded, and explored.

It is time now, dear ones. It is time.

The divine feminine has always been here. But it has not been recognized. It has been seen as a mystery and something to fear in ourselves because it could not be explained.

We the masters tell you again that you will not be seeing with your eyes, hearing with your ears, touching with your physical senses, that which is the unknown, the Hidden Source, which is the divine feminine.

You will be using your sixth sense, your inner knowing, for that is the only way that you will be able to know the divine fem-

inine, this unknown, unnameable place that you can feel, and sense, in the mother darkness.

It is in your sleep, in your dreams, that you will understand. It is in the hushed-breath magical moments that we have described.

It is time now for the sleeping dragon in the collective unconscious to become conscious, to awake to its ability to know, to sense, to rest in the safety and the boundless love of the unknown that is the divine feminine.

There is much here that will take time to understand. Allow yourselves to sink into the realm of dreams and the unknown and the mother darkness within each and every one of you.

Know that we love you and hold you in this dark realm. What is hidden is meant to be hidden. We the masters do not look to know ourselves. We do not look to reveal ourselves in this place.

And yet there is a deep reassuring knowing in this place—long held, long awaiting this time now—beginning to draw itself forth from out of the unconscious with these words today, so that the consciousness of the collective will begin to allow for the truth of this transmission.

Go in peace, beloveds, for you are the beloved, and you are on the path of the beloved, are you not?

Go in peace.

We love you. We hold you in this profound place.

Thank you for allowing us to speak today.

In the light and the mother darkness, we thank you.

I thank all that came and feel blessed to have received such beautiful messages and insights.

July 18, 2009

I am just now beginning to embrace the mother darkness, the divine feminine for myself.

Magdalen: *Your book about Yeshu was about a topic you already knew so much about. It was about the Great Love which you are, and his story that came so easily to you, as both live in the Revealed Source.*

Now you are delving into the hidden, the submerged, the darkness, where no light shines to show you the way.

What would have happened if my gospel had not been "lost" or "buried," as it was intentionally? What would have happened if I, in that lifetime, had been seen and heard as who I truly was, a white witch, a high priestess, for indeed that is who I was, sweet one. And when I say white witch, and when I speak of magic, dear ones, I want you all, dear readers, to hear this. I am not talking about spell-making or turning people into frogs. I am talking about recognizing the power of the unknown in all of us and tapping into it to allow for creation to occur.

The world of men was not prepared for my words then, nor was the world of women! No!

All is as it was meant to be. The persecutions of the Inquisition and the dominance of the Church of old played their part in bring-

ing all manner of things out of the dark into the open, beginning the release of those energies from the planet and the collective consciousness. The same is true for these war and scarcity issues surfacing and releasing now, making way for what is to come.

Men in power during the Inquisition and the old Church, and many others—women too—feared the unknown within themselves, and so denied it, and stamped out all that was hidden and unknown, in reaction.

They feared that which they saw around them: the ancient Judaic rituals, the healing powers of herbs and the women who used them, the profound faith of the Cathars^G—anything that was different from what they knew, because, unconsciously, they saw the hidden and the unknown within themselves reflected there.

They stamped all this out in the name of religion and a wrathful merciless God whom they had invented.

How long has humanity feared the unknown—the mother darkness, the divine feminine—in the belief that only the known is safe, since it is understood?

The Druidic priestesses in the British Isles understood. When I was there with Yeshu and after, without him, as we lay in the caves of initiation for the cycle of a moon, we understood what it was to lie in the dark unknown, and we reveled in the mystery of it and of the unknown within ourselves.

This is enough for now. We are so glad to spend so much time with you, dear one. Enjoy your gardening today!

Thank you, Magdalen, I say. *Thank you. It seems that the more I learn, the more there is to learn! And I am grateful for that and at the same time impatient!*

Magdalen: *Allow the timing and the timelessness of the divine feminine. Allow that what comes, comes exactly as it is meant to. I say this to all the readers now, about all issues in your life, dear ones. My blessings to you.*

7

RELEASING THE KARMIC BARGE

August 4, 2009

For some time, I've wanted to write a chapter called "Releasing the Karmic Barge," but I had no idea of its specifics. The time has come to write it now because I've been having a difficult time getting past something that feels not of this lifetime. I am hoping that, in the writing of it, something will shift for me.

I have wanted so much to feel good about renting my tiny cottage next door to my best friend, but for some reason I am in fear about it. My friend has nothing but loving, nonjudgmental energy about her. She's in the cottage now, having a personal retreat. She is the only one I trust enough to listen to my CDs—as they come—of these channelings. So I've been asking myself, what's wrong with me? Despite the times that I feel in my master self, I fall back to this place of judging myself and I don't want to do that anymore.

When I wake full of dreams, I forget them because I feel her presence instead in my energetic space, even though I can't see the cottage from my bed. She's only here for two days of retreat, and I love her, so why can't I do this?

I want to move through this karma that I am guessing revolves around my terror around abuse. I began this lifetime as an infant in a crib in Japan (where I was born), lying wet, hungry, cold, and alone, not knowing when I would be fed or changed, or held, or when someone would come in and hurt me.

I can't really explain how I know this about that time, other than the many body memories in which I experienced just that. I do know that I was taken care of by a Japanese nursemaid less than a decade after World War II ended, after America dropped atom bombs on Hiroshima and Nagasaki. How could any Japanese person be fond of an American in those days?

I know also that my father invaded me in those days, whether psychically or physically I cannot say for certain. All I can attest to is the spectrum of physical feelings I have experienced in my body when I allow myself to go back to that time, the stark terror of the door opening.

I believe that this feeling of energetic invasion into my force field—the field of energy around me that is mine alone—is related to lifetimes of abuse, persecution and the Inquisition, and I want to release it all. I want to just unhook the heaping barge of it that drags down my little sailboat so I can float freely down the river, on my path to freedom. Of course, I want it to be that easy. Who wouldn't?

But I don't know how to release it.

So, I call on Magdalen again, blindly, having to trust that she can help me through this, bringing with her the Magdalene energy that is connected to the divine feminine, the Mother, the masters, teachers, and Source, so that I can understand, and heal.

Perhaps some of you, dear readers, experience the same thing as I do. I have said that this channeling is just for me today, because I want to be free to blunder and grope and find my way, to allow the Magdalene energy to flood me with her love, her healing, and her teachings on this subject, without having to worry about what my readers may think. And yet, I have dared to include this channeling here, to offer myself as a mirror to others, as in this entire book.

I ask for assistance in releasing the barge, that I be easy on myself, and also that I find a way to move gently into this multidimensional person that I am becoming.

So, I now call upon Magdalen, the Magdalene energy, Yeshu, Vywamus, Germaine and Merlin, the faeries, devas, the divine feminine, the mother darkness, and too the beautiful energy of this land that holds me.

I call forth the Magdalene energy now, and it comes.

Magdalen: *Dear one. How well you sit with us here. You know that we love you.*

Today I come as the Magdalene energy that is the divine feminine, the Mother, the Hidden Source—all these, as well as the masters too. You have asked us here today to assist you in releasing what you call the karmic barge of abuse and trauma. Yes, it is the persecution energy of lifetimes, the Inquisition energy.

We ask that you allow us to step in now. We ask that you allow yourself to relinquish control of this channeling. We can feel your fear of losing control, your lack of safety. Are you not hypervigilant much of the time, unless you are alone? And is this not the issue now, with your friend perhaps renting the cottage, within sight of your house? Yes.

You question if you are going crazy. You ask if there is something wrong with you. You question your own feelings and you wonder, you doubt yourself.

Yes, we know this, do we not?

For this is the exact experience of self-doubt that occurred in the Inquisition, with its torture of those who knew, inside, what was true. Knowing what is true, and yet being told it is not.

You, as a small infant, lying in your crib in Japan. Yes, we were with you, my child, our child. We were with you then. We were holding you but there was so much terror and agitation in your small body that you could not feel our force fields around you. You could not feel that we were actually protecting you from worse abuse. You assumed, and rightly so, without conscious words or thought, that those who loved you would keep you safe, and this was not always true. So how could you trust your truth, dear one?

There you were, a small child, there in your crib, cold, hungry, alone, in terror, your body rigid, not knowing when it would be invaded. And, for you, not knowing when it would happen was the hardest to endure.

Did you not experience this same dread when you stuttered, as a child, as a teenager, and as an adult? For, in many lifetimes, it was not safe to speak your truth. For is not speaking your truth being truly who you are in all ways? Being free to allow your I-ness to shine, your entire being in alignment? What you say, wear, do, in every moment, in every breath of your daily life, internal and external?

It is that truth that comes from your inner knowing, even if it does not align with the truth of any other being. It is that truth that the persecutors of the Inquisition attempted to destroy in you. In not just this dimension, dear one. On not just this planet.

We are delighted that you have felt these feelings this morning. We are delighted that you have allowed yourself to truly feel the anguish and the seeming energetic invasion of your force field, which is an extension of your truth. For in feeling these feelings, they have come to the surface, have they not? They ask for release, do they not?

We hear your desire to have this beautiful woman as a neighbor. She who listens to our words with joy in her heart. She who creates gardens along with the devas and faeries, in love, in devotion, in humility, and in joy, blessing every plant, every flower, that she places in the ground.

We also understand your pain. This has been a struggle on this planet for lifetimes. From the very first moment that humanity incarnated on this earth, there was a struggle. Before that, there was the knowledge of light, the knowledge of Source and being Source. Upon incarnation into human body, there began a struggle between the effortless experience of pure being—energy, truth, light—and then suddenly having mass, body, individual personalities who differed and had their own energies and desires in physical space.

Somehow, for you, there is the fear that someone else's force field can intrude on yours, that someone else's truth can intrude on yours, and steal your soul. Is this not truly what you fear? Is it not your soul that you fear being harmed, here with your friend?

Allow yourself now to remember the lifetimes of persecution, being boiled in oil, hung by a rope, bound, gagged, strapped to the stone altar, your belly gouged, the armored soldiers standing by in the top of the tower, the Inquisition itself when you sat with blaring lights, strapped to the chair. The questions, questions, questions, and having no answers. Finally, giving up your truth in the hope that you might live.

The lifetime of the Cathar when you felt such joy in your light—we remember it with you now—and had no fear of the torture. And yet even in that lifetime, there was the memory in your body of the other lifetimes of persecution, on the edge of your energetic field, in your soul's eyes.

You have asked, what can you do to change this hypervigilance? We ask you to trust us and, even more, we ask you to trust yourself.

We feel the tears moving through your body. We feel your heart open in this moment, as we flood you with love, as your own love floods you. We know that you can release this karmic barge. We know this. We ask you, are you willing to release it? Are you willing to see it gone?

And yes, we see the word "hesitation" float by as if on that water that leads you to freedom. We ask again, are you willing to release this karmic barge? What do you fear in releasing it?

Yes, dear one, we hear your thoughts now. You fear the freedom of leaving that karmic barge behind, do you not? Will you be able to cry, will you be able to write, if there is no anguish? Dear one, do you truly believe that, as a human being, you will never feel anguish again? And is it only in anguish that your writing comes?

We are laughing in delight at your process. This is not in judgment, dear one. Not at all. This is a loving utterance from us who have been incarnate, for you know, as we do, that old energy releases in levels. We are giving you an invitation to release this karmic barge now, so that you can be free to move towards your freedom, even though other layers of flotsam and jetsam may surface later.

Will you embrace your freedom? Will you allow yourself to lie in the hammock in full view of your new neighbor?

We watch as you imagine yourself lying in that hammock and fearing her energy penetrating your force field. Can her energy truly penetrate your force field? In this moment, in your fear, will you open your heart and send love to your friend instead, and to yourself? Are you willing to allow yourself to be seen? Is this not the issue, dear one?

We feel the tears of truth moving through your chakra^G system. We see the tears of truth moving through your heart, through your solar plexus, into your belly now, as that truth lifts another layer of the old karmic wounds of being seen.

For invisibility renders painlessness, does it not, or so you have thought? When you are invisible, you cannot be tortured. That has been your belief. But is that the truth now? Lying in your bed this morning, you cannot see the cottage, your friend cannot see you, and yet you still feel the intrusion, like the persecution of those days.

The infant in her crib, even when she was not seen, when the door was closed, feared what would come, just as you fear what will come. We can feel the fear in your belly now, as we speak of this fear and terror. The old terror, the fears of the infant, the lifetimes of wanting to but not allowing yourself to speak your truth, going with the flow, going with what was expected of you so that you would be safe, invisible, accepted, and not persecuted, tortured, and destroyed.

This lifetime now is not those lifetimes. It is time now to allow yourself to be seen and to allow your truth to be heard. It is time now to move through that old karma, as you will, dear one, as you will. You will find your way. This is a certainty. It has already been written in your akashic records.^{G} You are already finding the way, in this unfolding now. Was it not the unknown, for the infant, that held the terror? Just as it is the unknown that has created fear in the collective consciousness until now, when it is time to allow the *divine feminine, deep within, to move into a spoken truth, known and recognized.*

We are not speaking of revealing what is hidden inside in the old ways that are known in this time now, using the five senses. Of what are we speaking? Let us make it clear for you.

We are speaking of honoring the magic and the power of your force field—of the truth of all that you know, of that which is deep and strong inside of you.

We are speaking of honoring, embracing, allowing yourself to shine in that force field! Know now that no one can invade or steal the soul of your truth.

Hear us now!

Your force field, your power, your magic, your truth, all of which are one—this is our power, our magic, our truth, our force field! Remember the divine consort? For are we not all Source, as one reflecting the all of Source itself? Believe this in this moment, dear one. Is this not so?

We feel the tears of this truth moving from your heart through your solar plexus to your belly, as the truth of this emerges and releases into your consciousness now.

The magic that is your force field, that is the divine feminine within you, the truth of your soul, all of the knowledge of your monadic consciousness: this is your heritage, dear one!

This is your force field!
This is your power!
This is your truth!

This is who you are!

Dare you assume—and I say this with love and support and all equality—that you are less than that? That you are less than those masters, what you humans call ascended masters, less than those masters who sit with me today? No one can steal our souls, dear one! No one!

The infant, the child inside, came in with the force field of your soul. We understand fully the karma that has brought you to this moment. We know with all of our hearts that, in your master self, you are as much master as we are, and that even these feelings of yours, which you share in all vulnerability with humanity, are beloved of us, and are a part of your unfolding.

Do you not see that it is the persecutions and all of those lifetimes that led you—that drove you—to want so desperately in this lifetime to speak and claim your truth, which is the power of who you fully are?

We ask you now, today, in this moment, to recognize that the fear that you feel around the unseen energy of your friend, in the cottage next door, is a fear that has been held in your cellular memory for lifetimes, in response to the abuse and persecution. It is the infant's dread in the crib in this lifetime that brought you the kinesthetic link to this moment now, so that you could release it.

Know this, sweet one. Know this.

In your wisdom you know that, in the soul place before this lifetime, you called in the abuse that you experienced as an infant, so that it would trigger you to finally clear all abuse for all lifetimes, past, present, future, and parallel, backwards and forwards to the divine plan of your soul, all the way to the time when you were newly sparked from Source.

And when we speak to you, dear one, we hope all who read this, will understand that we speak to all humanity. We speak also to the collective consciousness whose time it is to release all of that old karma of abuse and subsequent fear. This planet too has the desire to release her own karmic barge.

This planet has already begun the clearing of the persecutions, the Inquisitions, the tortures against speaking the truth of that which is deep within, of the divine feminine.

As the Magdalene energy of the divine feminine, I was there with Sonanda,^{G} as we created this beautiful planet. We saw the entire revolution of fear, wars, pestilence, scarcity—all of this that was to come. All of these issues went back to the original monadic misunderstanding of separation, which we are clearing now. For with the certainty of all beings being loved by Source since creation, would there have been war or famine or scarcity?

Dear one, you do this for all.

Wrap yourself in the robes of all that you are. Don the majesty of your force field. Own it. Place the crown on your head. Stand tall. Own this force field of your magic, your truth, your mastery.

Throw the old fears into the karmic barge, even if you doubt this movement. Know that this is letting go of layers, and there may or may not be more. The masters are here in this moment supporting you in this. Fill the barge to heaping, if that's what it takes. Add another barge if you need to. Add barges to the nth power if you need to see them that way.

You may also just (snaps her fingers) *throw them away in an instant, for you know that you have the power to do this. Trust yourself. Trust us. Allow that the fear can go as easily as it comes.*

Give yourself this gift, dear one.

Allow yourself now to move into a place where you are truly willing to release this karmic barge. Allow yourself to settle into this place with your robes and your crown.

Give your inner children a faery wand! Surround yourself with the devas, the faeries, the angelic realm, and with us, the ascended masters who love you. Allow yourself to open your heart and, with your heart full open, in your beaming, streaming, light-filled glory, allow yourself to reach over. Touch the latch—the link, the tow bar— of that karmic barge and, with your heart open in the knowledge of the magic of all that you are, and with our blessings and our faith in you, as your faith in yourself, let that karmic barge go NOW!

Watch it as it drifts farther and farther away, as you sail forward faster and faster on your path to freedom, dear one.

On your path of freedom! Knowing that you can. Knowing that this is your heart's desire. Knowing that this life is yours to live fully.

Blessings, dear ones, all of you who have done this for yourselves. Blessings to you. We love you and applaud you! And those who have read these words and have not seen themselves releasing the barge, know that, if it is in alignment with your highest Source Self, know that it is done.

There is a beating of wings as the angelic realm hovers close by. There is much gladness here, as you walk now in the robes and the crown of your own well-deserved majesty.

Blessings to you now.
In peace and joy, we leave you for now.

Just after the channeling, I am filled with the joy of this freedom. I walk past the cottage and feel no intrusion. Later, I look out the kitchen window at my garden and straight at the cottage, and I still feel no intrusion whatsoever, of anyone else's energy.

Later still, I go out to the hammock to read in complete comfort, even though I am in full view of the cottage windows!

What can I say?
Thank you!

8

ALLOW YOUR SMALLNESS

August 16, 2009

Ever since channeling the previous chapter, I have felt a nagging feeling that I unintentionally let my inner children down, by denying their fears around my friend moving into the cottage next door.

If I am to treat myself as a beloved, how can I deny my feelings? How can I deny the feelings of my inner child? Does my channeling to joy and freedom, without embracing the feelings of the inner child, effect any permanent change? If the inner child feels shamed, silenced, how can there be room for the joy and freedom?

I know there is a way to reconcile this, and even Magdalen brings it up in her words here that she whispered to me this morning when I asked her about it.

Magdalen: *My Beloved Yeshu wrote a chapter called "Allow Your Greatness."*[7] *I would offer that you, sweet ones, also allow your smallness. Listen to the child within. Listen to your teens. Allow that there are times when you want to hide, or be invisible, or lie in bed with the covers over your head, or do nothing at all!*

What I want to do is embrace the joy and teachings of the masters, as well as the feelings of the child in the crib. What I don't want to do is to feel disappointment in myself for any feeling I have. There is no such thing as a bad feeling or a good feeling. All feelings have value. Naming them allows me to embrace them, and even saying that I don't want to feel them allows me to embrace that also.

I know that all healing occurs in layers and that, yes, there is a layer of permanent change effected from the previous release and every time that I re-read it. At the same time, the nagging is still here, and I want to learn more about this.

I just came back from a beautiful walk along the brook, around the corner from my house, and through the farm, to the sounds of rushing water, cows bellowing in the fields, and a phoebe on the wire. I realize that, for me, this is an important part of my life, connecting with the beauty of this planet that I have loved.

How blessed I am that I can take this walk. I think now of how Magdalen spoke in her story of belonging to all that is around her. That is how I feel walking in nature, as if I recognize and learn myself there, knowing that it heals me in some way. Doing it with intention is one of the ways that I walk the path of the beloved, for I am treating myself with love when I do so. I also know that my inner child delights in the sounds and the scents and the feel of the walk, with me. All of these sensations feel in alignment with me and soothe the child in me.

Speaking with my friend again about renting my cottage, I told her, I don't want to push this rental. In that moment, I realized that that indeed was what I had been doing. I had been pushing myself into doing something that denies who I am.

Why can't I simply honor my force field for what it is, and know that who I am needs all this room, to the farthest bounds of my land, so that I can be and write and evolve? I love the purity of my force field when I am alone. It feels important for my life and the writing of these books. Why can't I simply allow for who I am, in all of my facets?

I am realizing that there is a fine line between hypervigilance—as a result of lifetimes of abuse, fear, pain, and the persecutions of the Inquisition—and sensitivity, in an awareness of the presence of "other," be it another person, or irritating noise or sensation, that intrudes on my need to focus, in the presence of myself alone.

I want clarity on this so I ask Magdalen, and she answers.

Magdalen: *I am Magdalen. Mother Mary is with me, alongside of me. How we love your courage to speak your own story as the story of all, and we love all parts of you.*

When we speak of allowing your smallness, are we not speaking of allowing the voices of the small ones inside? Are we not speaking of cradling them in our arms? Our hearts open with love, with the tears of joy of a new mother, as we rock and cradle each and every dear small one, inside of each and every one of you, our readers.

For is not the awareness of the incremental feeling, emotion, experience—is that not precious, dear ones? Is that awareness not an allowing that is also part of the divine feminine, the mother within? Is it not a form of cradling in itself?

Yes, dear ones. Yes, we rock you in our arms. Two Marys together, we rock you in our arms. There is so much love here.

Is not the small child still close to the light time—when all was energy and light? There is a free-flowing unconscious expectation of the same beauty and joy and giftedness as the light time from which it came, every feeler out, every cell wide awake and expectant. That is the experience, is it not, of the newborn human incarnate?

This newborn has no words, no experience of self, is fully alive, fully present in a state of pure beingness—every cell, every molecule alive and present to the abundance of life around it.

At some point, early on, comes what may be called an abrasion substance—acting as an abrasive to the light time experience that the newborn lives and expects. Perhaps it is an older brother who shouts in anger, or a mother whose energy of overwhelm travels the frequencies to the newborn's feelers. Perhaps it is someone even more intrusive, dear ones.

Over time, after repeated interaction with the abrasion substance, an expectation grows—a hypervigilance, if you will—that asks, without words, without conscious thought, when will this come again? This that is like sandpaper to the purity of my force field?

The sensations of this hypervigilance may be increased pulse, held breath, sharpened hearing, rigidity in the extremities, perhaps even numbness and leaving the body.

These sensations in response to the abrasion substance embed into the cellular memories and then are triggered automatically, the next time some abrasion substance, even unconsciously perceived, presents itself to you.

For some like you, dear channel, and many who read these words, this sensitivity is very prominent in life. Many and many who read these words are still very close to the light time, or have come very close again because of their desire to be conscious. And for many, there is judgment that something is wrong with the self.

Know now that that sensitivity that stirs your cells is part of the awakening that allows you to embrace yourself fully. It asks of you that you take note of what you feel, and honor it, listen to what it is telling you. To do so is to treat yourself as a beloved, dear ones.

As the collective consciousness begins to bring its unconscious awareness into consciousness, the more of you will be embracing a multidimensional awareness of the unnamed parts of yourself that have, until now, been hidden. You will begin to notice and allow, know and nurture those parts, as Source sought to know itself in you.

Imagine, if you will, that the newborn human in its purest state is the entire realm of Hidden Source, the mystery, the unknown, the unknowable. And then come all the divergent and individual facets of the outer life of the known.

Are you not moving and evolving into your multidimensional awareness? It is this awareness that is sensitive to minute energies, to minute variations in the frequencies and the vibrations around you, as well as within the nuances of emotion, and interaction, and sensation, which comprise the human being.

For this channel, even in her questioning of this book in which she speaks out loud her personal experience, there is a knowing that this is what she must do. It is her very sensitivity that brings forth her multidimensional experience, and by allowing and honoring it, she both enhances her multidimensionality and treats herself as a beloved.

And you also, beloved readers, there are many and many of you, who want this for yourselves.

Gift yourselves by allowing this sensitivity. Rejoice in it. Allow yourselves to discern the difference between hypervigilance, which is fear, and sensitivity, which is knowing. Knowing with absolute certainty that what you feel is true. It does not have to be true for anyone else.

Allow your smallness. Allow the small, incremental feeling, the trace, the particle of awareness inside of you that says: This is not right for me. I feel that I am pushing this, or there is something about this that I don't like. I am attracted to this more than that.

I feel good when I eat this, not as good when I eat that. I am hungry in this moment. I am glad that I have fed myself. I am aware that I am tired, and yet I also want to read for a few minutes longer, still aware that I am tired, knowing that I will also sleep when I am ready.

We have shifted, have we not? The incremental awareness: my body needs rest now. My body needs food now. My body needs exercise now. I am hungry. I am tired. I need fresh air. I am lonely. I want to speak with a friend. Who can I call?

What do I need in this moment?

How can I gift myself in this moment?

As the channel walks on the road through the farm, feeling the wind and the air, delight in the bird song, the mountain view, the streams, the wild flowers, the oneness that she feels as part of this planet, the doe's whoof as she sniffs the grass....

Each one of these sensations is a particle of the "smallness," is an incremental part of the beloved of the self. Allow yourselves, dear ones, to treat every incremental particle of yourselves, as beloved.

When you embrace your sensitivity, you also expand it. You give it permission to expand your experience of it.

Dear ones, there is no need to judge the sensitivity. When there is fear combined with this sensitivity, when the hypervigilance comes, cradle that part that feels the hypervigilance. Kiss the forehead. Stroke the hair. Feel us here with you, loving you. Do not judge it, dear ones. Instead, allow yourselves, perhaps, to reframe the hypervigilance term, to one of sensitivity and ask yourselves, what do I want here? What is truly right for me here? How can I make this work for me?

How can I live my life fully, treating myself as a beloved, in grace, and in alignment with my own force field, which is moving into this multidimensionality of which we have spoken.

Allow yourselves to bring in your divine masculine^G ability of discernment to precision-tune your need—your awareness—of your knowing. Use the tools you are born with, dear ones. Use all the tools you have, for they become more and more available to you, as clarity comes. And clarity also is a part of the divine masculine, is it not?

The channel feels her awareness opening even now. Her third eye opens in this moment, as if her force field is expanding. Dear readers, allow this for yourselves also. We are opening and expanding the field, to include now facets of the divine masculine in consciousness. For you need both. And there will be a day when the word "both" will dissolve and become merely divine awareness, and the all that you truly are.

Every moment that you are aware of the microscopic particles of your experience, you expand into the multidimensional experience of Source itself, and thus into your own Source Self.

We are feeling much movement here. There is a vibrational shift in the channel, and in the place where we sit, from these words. Vywamus is here. Source sits right here with us. Yeshu is here too.

Allow our immense love for you. Open your heart of hearts to the experience of the tiny fragile newborn inside each and every one of you, and allow the light time to shine through. Allow the time even before light to bring you to the very breadth of your experience.

We welcome each and every one of you as you assist in this evolution of the collective consciousness to own its multidimensional awareness, and its multidimensional sensitivity.

We shall leave you now, but know that we love you, always.

We honor you in your journeys, on your paths. We honor each and every one of you, with so much gratitude for your willingness, dear ones, to walk the path of the beloved with us, with each other, and with yourselves.

Allow each and every particle of your inner experience the room for acknowledgment, for each is a particle of Source itself, the beautiful force field that is the divine in all of its glory.

Go in peace now, with our love and our gratitude.

Go in peace.

This channeling had a different tone and feeling for me. It feels very soft, gentle, loving. Magdalen felt closer to the earth plane and sat side by side on the couch with Mother Mary.

I now understand that honoring all my feelings, whether fear, shame, joy, or freedom, is part of being a multidimensional being, part of treating myself as a beloved. I now see that, when I accept that I simply do not want a neighbor, I am honoring who I am.

Thank you, Beloveds, for your wisdom and unending gifts.

9

ALLOWING LOVE IN

August 29, 2009

How can I create a loving mother within, if I never experienced one outside of myself, at least not until the last two months of my mother's life? And why is it that I need to get all the big should-things done, before I can feel safe? Why do I feel so anxious about them?

Yesterday, I came to a decision—its content irrelevant here—over which I've been feeling anxious, tired, and weepy with the stress of it. Now, today, my first day off—that is, alone—in a week, I tell myself I have to channel, simply because I have the time to do it.

It occurs to me to ask, why? Who says?

Why do I need to talk this over with Magdalen, as if I can't come up myself with the simple fact that I am allowed to take the whole day off, let myself catch up if I want to, play, clean my room, swim in the rain, whatever?

My mother's house is selling in four weeks. There's a twisted ball of attorneys and co-trustees and investors to comb through before I can get to the simple fabric of my life. I've taken on the purchase of a cottage in Rockport, Massachusetts, near the ocean—for joy, and the tears of rightness that come every time I talk with the realtor about it.

But did I have to agree to having the bulkhead re-painted this weekend? Do I have to channel Magdalen today? There is so much else I'd like to do with my time and, then—if I feel like it—I can channel her.

Somehow, there's a part inside that I feel should be here but seems to be missing.

It's the part that says, Good girl, what a great job you did. I'm so impressed with you for how you persevered and came to exactly the right decision. I know how hard that was and how much it took out of you. What you decided feels so good, so full of integrity, so safe for everyone inside. Good for you! You deserve a big reward! You deserve to rest on the laurels of what you did, to really take in what you did for yourself. You deserve to give yourself a day to rest and play after all that.

But that hasn't been my way. That wasn't my mother's way. When I called her up twenty years ago to tell her I finally got my masters degree, the first words out of her mouth were, So when are you going to get your doctorate?

I know this is somehow related to my being unable to take in my therapist's hugs, or her words of love. At least until the other day.

The child in me was angry at her and testing her love, and feeling that she'd betrayed me, because it didn't seem she was hearing me or fulfilling my needs. Her seeming betrayal validated my old belief that, if I ask for something, I'll make mommy—or whoever I put in that mommy role in the moment—angry. Then she will reject me or, even worse, ignore me so that I'll feel completely abandoned and unloved.

At least, says the skewed and shrewd little voice inside, if I don't ask for anything, I won't be rejected.

But when I walk into my therapist's office, and I see all the flowers she's set out for our session, and the two mugs of tea that she makes only for me, I start to weep. A thick hard lifetimes-old knot—made up of hurt and rejection, and the knowledge that, if I speak my truth, I will be rejected, even killed—starts to soften, as it soaks in the bath of my tears.

I keep testing her—barely looking at her—daring to tell her I've been angry at her, feeling like strangling her and shaking her and calling her stupid, the way I wanted to call my mother stupid and my father stupid for not seeing and valuing who I was, and for leaving me unprepared for being a "grown-up" in this life!

I tell her my adult knows I'm projecting my biological mother onto her, but at the same time, the child can't seem not to feel these feelings about her.

My therapist is honest, and she tells me, yes, she had reacted to something I had said in the last session. She was authentic with me.

She's not like my mother who lived behind a wall, even when, at the age of twelve, I screamed at her every bad name I could think of, to get her to show me her feelings—angry or hurt, or anything at all. Somehow, if she had, I would have known that I could have an impact on her, that I mattered.

But all my mother did was smile smugly, and walk away. I can still feel the punch in my belly even though, now, I can understand. She herself was hurting and didn't know how to say so.

As I weep in my therapist's office, I feel the tears soften another layer off that hard leather knot of my own wall inside—like my mother's—that I have built over lifetimes. The wall that says, it's not safe to trust anyone. It's not safe to allow love in because, if I allow love in, I'll be hurt, as with Mom and Dad—and all the men I've been with—and my earlier friends, and past lives, because that is what I have known.

No wonder it's been such a struggle and so psychically huge to deal with the "trusts" our mother left us, when the word itself is antithetical to the reality that she didn't trust us at all.

Somehow, this girl-child that I was, this woman-child that I am, this beautiful being, so precious and light-filled, spoke her truth to a therapist—another human being—and came to a surprising place! I was able to take in, experience in my body and heart, in my whole being, my therapist's loving embrace.

I realize now that my anxiety this morning around getting all the should-things done was really not about them at all. It was about putting the should-things first and leaving unsaid and unprocessed, all of this movement in my psyche around my therapist and my birth mother, and allowing love in, at last.

What I really need is to be with myself, as I am doing now. The habit of moving on before I've processed what I've just experienced, is my mother's way of responding to me—hurrying me, not attending—which doesn't move me forward at all.

By writing here, allowing myself to take this in, I am invoking my own loving mother within. I am held in my own loving embrace. I am loving myself, without pushing a huge internal movement under the rug. I am building trust in myself and applauding myself for listening to my own truth by not attending to the should-things instead.

I close my eyes and a big sigh of healing moves through me, like a gentle wave of warm ocean water. I feel like I am putting on new internal clothes, as my loving mother within moves more into form.

The leather knot softens further. Finally, the anxiety of days is abating. I can feel the healing move across lifetimes and centuries, back to my soul's divine plan. There is the feeling that I am not alone and, yet, physically, I am. It is my own loving mother within who accompanies me.

I am learning to trust myself. This is huge. And I am learning to love myself from the inside.

I thank my psyche for this day, for carving out this time for me and for insisting that we turn off the phone and put cloths over the message light so I don't even have to think about another human being!

I thank my loving mother within for gently nudging me. And of course my beloved team of masters who are always here with me.

10

LOVING MOTHER WITHIN

August 31, 2009

It is amazing to me how I struggle between the developing loving mother within and the introjected,[G] overwhelmed mother that lurks in my psyche. It's like living in a constant battle. On one side, I want to actively nurture myself—feed myself, bathe, go for walks. On the other side is the looming group of things that I need to or should get done—my daily chores that often fill me with resentment even though they take care of my life and my home.

I am feeling frustrated because (and now the tears come, in my heart and my solar plexus) I really want to take care of myself, and at the same time I want to get things done. How do I pace this path, avoid feeling a huge sense of impending doom, if I don't get all "hundred" things—exaggerated, of course—done today, at the expense of taking care of myself?

Who wins? My internalized overwhelmed mother, or the loving mother within?

I can do some of the things on the list. I can feed my birds and my plants. I usually go for a walk, or a swim in the morning—something to keep my body moving so it stays flexible.

I just don't understand why it is so hard. Or maybe I do. I know that I lived with a mother who resented taking care of us children. When she braided my hair in the mornings before school, she would just yank the comb through it, not even holding the top, instead of starting at the bottom and working up. I know she was overwhelmed, with five children to raise by herself. This is not about blame. This is about wanting to do things differently, wanting to learn how to really care for myself. When I say that, grief washes through me.

There are too many details, too many directions in life. I want to do one thing at a time and, at the same time, I want to allow for the list of a hundred things, if that's what it is.

I want to see the list without the impending sense of doom, or something looming over me, that says it all has to be done RIGHT NOW, in order for me to feel safe. I know that that's what this is about, feeling safe. I also know that when I look at the list from the point of view of the soul, there seems to be a sense of peace, but I am still looking for more answers, more understanding on this.

This morning, I am doubting that Magdalen will come. Of course, she's already here, and the masters are here. The minute

I said that, of course they all flooded in. I really cannot imagine how I could possibly have walked this path without the masters, without Magdalen and all of the varied facets of the divine feminine who have come in to assist, guide, love, and support me, and I thank them all now again.

But will my questions be answered? Will I come to a place of peace? Will it change me? Will it affect me?

So, I am starting this channeling in a place of doubt. Not so much in my own abilities, but in Magdalen's abilities. In the abilities of the masters who are light, to answer a question from someone who has three-dimensional human lists, concerns, life!

Again, I call forth the most beautiful pure white crystalline light of the highest healing order. I ask for this light to surround me in a sphere of its light. I call forth the part of me that is able to channel, clearly and objectively, so that the "I" who has these concerns can stay out of the way.

I am getting a sense that it may or may not be Magdalen that comes today, or she may be a spokesperson for all the masters, rather than the Magdalene energy speaking for the planet, or the divine feminine. I think she speaks more for the loving mother within, for the Mother herself.

And again, tears fill my heart.

Magdalen: *We are here with you now, dear one. And yes, we the masters are all here speaking to you. Mother Mary is here, Yeshu. I* *look around the circle: St. Germaine,^G the vibration of Vywamus, Raphael,^G Michael,^G with his legions behind, the Lady Gaia^G holding cupped in her hands the queens of the devas and faeries that live here on your land.*

And we speak now for the loving mother within you. We bring her in now and, yes, dear channel, we feel your immense tears, in your heart, in your voice. For it is your loving mother within who wishes to speak today, who wishes to speak for all the loving mothers within all of those who read this chapter.

Loving mother within: *Know now, dear ones, that we are here with each and every one of you. We are embedded in your being. We are embedded in your heart. We watch your struggle.*

We hold the children, all of the inner children in our embrace. Our arms reach wide enough for all the ages of the children in our loving embrace. Our breasts are wide enough and soft enough and great enough, to allow for the heads of all the little children to lean into us, as we stroke their sweet faces, as we stroke your sweet, soft hair.

And know this, dear ones. Know this now: Every tiny increment of what you do for yourself is an action of our love for you, is an action of the loving mother within's love for each and every part of you.

And, sweet children! Do you know that you cannot possibly love incorrectly? You cannot possibly nurture incorrectly!

You speak about the battle between the loving mother within and the overwhelmed mother introject. Dear sweet children, do you not know that the loving mother within holds the overwhelmed mother introject to her breast also?

Did not Yeshu, who is here sitting with us, speak of judgment, and loving the part which judges?[8] *Is this not like that?*

Ah, sweet souls. Sweet, sweet children. We watch you lovingly as you feel that you flounder. When you run and stumble and fall, do we pick you up every time? Of course not! We allow you the freedom and the sense of your own independence to pick yourself up, to gain strengths for yourself.

Dear channel, we watch you struggle through this very important piece of your own evolution, as the evolution of the collective consciousness and the planet herself. Is it not so?

We loving mothers within are always here with you. We embrace you, as you grow. Even in your tantrumming "terrible two-ness," when you reject us and turn from us, we are always here for you. Dear ones, precious children, we never leave you.

What you are doing, dear channel, and many others, is learning that you are important, that nurturing yourself is important, that you are no longer a slave tied to the old ways of the three-dimensional world of shoulds. Of course, there is learning here. Of course, there is struggling. Of course, there is stumbling and falling and picking yourselves up, as you try something new.

The struggle itself, the internal battle itself, dear ones, is actually the angst of change. Is it not? Many of you are no longer tied to the shoulds of society, and you are finding ways to replace those shoulds with the infinite possibilities of what you might want as a multidimensional being, the new human who fully loves himself or herself.

Dear ones, we ask for you to know in all of your being that the masters are here for you. Magdalen, Mother Mary, Yeshu, Vywamus, all of us, the devas, the faeries, the angelic realm. There is so much support for you here, so much.

So, when you get lost in the jungle of three-dimensional shoulds—the lists, the tangles of the three-dimensional world—when you find that you have forgotten to feed yourself, or walk in nature, or perhaps you have chosen not to walk because there were so many things on your list—dear ones, you need not blame yourself.

You need not blame yourself for not having completed all the "tasks of necessary nurturing," for does that then not put the realm of self-care into the box of tangles of the three-dimensional world of lists and shoulds?

Sweet, precious children! Allow that there is room for everything. Allow that there is time for everything. Allow that the soul's body, your multidimensional body, does not have a time schedule.

The channel is getting a headache now thinking about all those things that she feels that she must do daily, in order to truly love herself, in order to truly have an "evolved" loving mother within.

Sweet channel. It is true that you have not known an external loving mother. You believe that you must create this internal loving mother to be absolutely perfect.

So let me see what the list would be of the "perfect" loving mother within. Let's hear the thoughts of the channel, and say them out loud as we hear them: the perfect loving mother within should make sure that the channel gets eight hours of sleep per day, does not snack in bed at night, does her physical therapy twice a day, goes for at least an hour walk or an hour swim in the morning.

Let's see, anything else? Does anything else come? Ah, yes. She makes juice every morning, eats raw vegetables, juices for herself at night, has a salad every night, has protein in the middle of the day, so she does not get overwhelmed with the wrong amount of food, shouldn't drink her espresso in the morning (although she refuses not to drink her espresso in the morning!).

Oh, my goodness. My goodness! We have created a taskmaster, have we not?

Let me tell you, my sweet channel, and all of our readers. Let me tell you about the true loving mother within.

First of all, if one should attach the word "perfect," then the word "perfect" should be attached to all beings. Or we may simply throw that word out. Gone! Thank you.

Dear ones, dear children. There is a rumbling of dread within the inner children of this channel, believing it is their duty to create the perfect loving mother within, that they should know how to do this. Perhaps many and many who read this, believe that they too should know how to do this.

Dear ones, we are creating here something new! We are not creating the loving mother within from the blueprints of the lifetimes already lived by the channel and so many others, where there was no concept of loving or nurturing the self.

The lifetimes of the queen who was served in all ways, do not come in to the making of a loving mother within. The loving mother within is NOT a queen, nor does she expect her children to serve her or comply with her "requirements" in all or any ways.

The lifetimes of the starving, thin, rag-clad beggar, do not come in. (The fear of the channel is that, if she is hungry and does not eat immediately, she is not loving herself, has not invoked the loving mother within and, therefore, she has failed and will die of starvation.)

The lifetimes of the Amazon tribal chieftess, the queen of the matriarchal societies, the planetary logos^G—those lifetimes in which the responsibility for many came before the self, those do not come in. This lifetime is for putting your own needs first.

Dear ones, as I have said, we are here creating something new, within the channel's psyche, within the collective consciousness of all humanity, for this planet, all planets and all universes.

Let me give you an image that is true, and we bring this image, here, now, into form. This image is something that many and many have glimpsed, scattered across the lifetimes and yet have not recognized as the loving mother within.

I am big and soft. My bosom is ample. My belly is round and soft, as are my arms and thighs. I am perhaps like the Goddess of Willendorf^G in the shape and form of my body. I hold my arms out wide. There is room for every single age of every inner child to sit in my lap, to lay his or her head on my breasts.

I comfort.

I listen.

I hear.

I mirror back.

I allow.

I hear you tell me that you are hungry and I say, yes, dear one. Yes, you are hungry. And when you are ready to eat, you will eat. And we will be with you when you are eating.

The channel asks me to explain to those who perhaps do not understand about all the ages of the inner children. In many humans, there are emotional reactions—triggers—like "inner buttons" being pushed that often go back to a certain experience in the childhood.

For instance, one of those experiences may have occurred at the age of three. If that experience was traumatic enough to the child, it may have frozen that particular three-year-old experience into the cells, locking it into cellular memory. That memory then stays in the cells, exactly as perceived, in the form of a frozen inner child, despite the age of the adult that that child becomes.

That locked frozen moment continues to trigger an emotional reaction to similar experiences in the adult, until that frozen moment is healed and cleared. If there are other ages at which traumas occurred, the moments of those traumas and the ages at which they occurred are also locked in the cells.

The trauma does not have to be big or horrifying to the adult mind. A child sees differently. Innocence and purity and light are its standards, its baseline.

Unless the three-year-old living that frozen moment again inside the adult is given the opportunity to feel the feelings of that moment, while being loved and held by the adult or someone else, that frozen moment does not heal. Instead, it stays with the soul in cellular memory through lifetimes.

Dear ones, know now that the frozen moments brought into this life are meant to be cleared for all times. Such is the time now, in humanity's evolution.

So, here I am in my great bulk, I the loving mother within. My ample bosom, my ample soft arms, my ample thighs. The cheeks of the little ones lie against the comforting softness of my skin. They have the tactile experience of the warmth of my body that feeds them.

I hear your wants, your dreams, your wishes. I hear your longings, your overwhelm, your panic. I hear your frantic desire to complete the entire list today. And I hold you in this.

Who I truly am, is an emanation of the Hidden Source, the divine feminine that holds all in mystery and love, and in deep and absolute devotion. Know this now. Hear these words.

There are no lists, no shoulds, no words, no content, nothing but the deep, rich, silent, gentle, all-encompassing love of the mother darkness, the unknown fathoms within you and within all that is the Mother.

Know that I do not judge you if you do not eat your breakfast in the first pang of hunger. You are not doing it wrong. I am not doing it wrong by not feeding you.

I am you learning the baby steps towards listening, recognizing, acknowledging what you truly want. I am you learning who *you are, combing through the tangle of the lists of all you want to do, and finding for yourself what feels right for you in the moment.*

So, dear ones, do not berate yourselves, and if you do, love that part too. Allow your berating, your angst, and your struggle as part of your falling down and picking yourself up. For you are learning a new process of having a loving mother within, of voicing and heeding what it is that you truly want in the moment.

And if it's that you want to make the list, so be it! If it's that you want to push through your stuckness, or frozen moment, loving yourself around braiding your hair, rather than pushing that aside, if that's what you want for yourself, so be it! If what you want is to feed your birds, and take the extra time to fill the feeder too, so be it! Let that be what you do in the moment.

If you want to rage and scream because it's all too hard and you don't know how to do it and you are angry at me for even suggesting this idea, so be it! But love the part that rages. And if you cannot consciously do this, then know that I love that part for you.

Dearest ones, I am here, your loving mother within. I am here to tell you that whatever you truly want to do in the moment, is exactly right for you. I am here to listen, to hear, to allow you—in every increment of your experience—to find your path, even if that path is one centimeter, one sixteenth of an inch at a time. Know that every increment of that path, whether you stumble, panic, brush your teeth, feel harried, take a walk, enjoy the outdoors, watch a movie—whatever you do on your path—I cherish, is cherished by all of us here.

For we know that you are moving through change.

Perhaps if you know that the loving mother within is here and available and working right alongside you—breathing, living, being within you—perhaps if you know this, then you can simply ask yourself, what is it that I truly want to do, right in this moment?

For in asking that question, dear ones, in asking that question of yourselves, you are actually living your three-dimensional, list-filled lives from a multidimensional view. For you are then seeing from the soul place, from the place where the masters sit, from the place where you as master live.

In recognizing that you are panicked and overwhelmed, that there are too many things on the list but you want to get it all done today because then you will be free, even though the lists continue every day—the recognition itself is your soul recognizing you.

When you recognize what you are doing, you are coming from the place of the master within, the place of the loving mother within, that is the multidimensional being that notices and is conscious of whatever incremental, infinitesimal experience you have.

For, dear ones, do you not know that the fifth dimensional plane—that of the soul—and other dimensional planes could snap a finger, and accomplish all in one split second?

Why do you think you have come into a three-dimensional body? It is partly so that you may experience this transition of loving yourself in body, moment to moment, to anchor it on this planet, for all planets, for all universes.

Of course, the Great Love pervades all. Of course, all beings are loved. But we are moving to the next step now. We are shifting to the state of being in which all beings allow, recognize, acknowledge, and embrace every incremental part of themselves, in love.

So, dear ones, precious children, allow yourselves to stumble and fall. Allow yourselves to rise. Allow yourselves every incremental, infinitesimal step of transition into this new state of firmly anchored love for yourself, that is Source's love within, that is the divine mother within. For is not the loving mother within the divine feminine itself? Of course.

We are speaking of allowing, acknowledging, appreciating and embracing each incremental, infinitesimal step, each pace, of the path. I say this again and again to embed it.

Make a list when it feels right. Eat when it feels right. Go to sleep at 8:30 at night if you wake up at 4:30 in the morning. How lovely to get eight hours of sleep. Or stay up till midnight and wake at 3 a.m., if that is what your being wants.

Listen to yourself. Allow that each step of your path is precious to me, and allow it to be precious to yourself as well. Hold each step, each emotion—the panic, the peace, whatever it is—hold it to my ample breast within you and love it. There is so much love for you here, within yourselves. For are you not multidimensional beings who hold Source inside of you, at all times?

Dear ones, we bless you for all times, and we thank you for being the vanguards of this transition, this new way of being.

We thank the channel for her willingness, her honesty, and her doubt, this morning. Even the doubt, allow. For is Source not used to the doubt of many?

Sweet ones, I leave you now. But know that you are precious to us, in all ways, at all times.

Go in peace.

I feel so held, so completely held.

As I channeled the loving mother within, I felt the width of her thighs, her arms, her breasts, as if they were mine. I felt her love filling me. I felt so completely blessed with the awareness of her love, made physical within me.

I feel hopeful, that I have truly begun to anchor her into my being. (Re-reading this in my final edit, I know that this is true for me now. She is a part of me, and I know that this experience, this channeling, helped me to begin to find her within myself.)

Thank you, Beloveds.

Thank you.

11

JUST FEELING

October 1, 2009

There is something so sacred about just feeling. Not criticizing, judging or analyzing the feelings, but just feeling them. Allowing the waves and waves of feelings to move through the body, especially through the second chakra and solar plexus to the heart and throat and knowing that, with each wave, the frozen child within is thawing.

Knowing that the child within is at last safe enough to feel. I say "safe enough" because I sometimes do not feel completely safe within my body, and I know others feel this way too. When I learned years ago in a hypnotherapy internship to take clients to a safe place, it was always a "safe enough" place instead, for this very reason. Saying "safe enough" lets the inner children know that there is nothing wrong with them if they do not feel completely safe yet. Whatever they feel is exactly right.

And it is the feeling that matters. The child is somehow aware that I am witness, that the loving mother within exists, no matter how ethereal she may seem, and she allows and witnesses and honors the feelings for what they are.

No need to ask what the feelings are. No need to describe or name them or even write them down in the moment.

Just noticing them, allowing the waves to pass through and, at the same time, feeling such silent hidden joy for and awe at the courage of the inner child who is at last expressing, after a lifetime of numbness.

There is gratitude here. There is release. There is newness and surprise that I don't have to do anything but allow, witness, and honor.

In the past, I thought I could only feel close to the feelings—live in the body of the child that I was—from within my three-dimensional self, rather than my master self. I thought that if I were in my master self, I would be somewhat separate from and "above" these feelings, which are so very important.

I know now that it is only within the master self, which is the multidimensional self, that I can be both loving mother within and inner child at the same time, accessing all that Source and the universe give to me. I readily allow and delight in the expansion of this new awareness and way of being.

October 3, 2009

Sometimes, all I can do is say "hit hit hit hit hit" and sob and sob and sob. Sometimes, the feelings of frustration, banging against the walls of the cage, get too big, and I finally remember that I am feeling, at last, the rage and impotence of the child.

I wrote a poem about this in 1995 after leaving everything I knew in California, and moving from the ocean that I loved and where I had lived for twenty-three years, to the woods of New England. I include the poem here.

I Can Describe the Box

I can describe the box in detail,
Its hard cold gray steel slats,
The rough-torn slots in the too-tight screws,
The sloppy thick weld marks at the corners,
The absence of a door,
The foot-and-a-half of space above me,
The two feet to either side and around me,
The empty echo of my voice which no one hears,
The way the slats cut into me
When I lean or sit or kneel or curl or crawl or stamp my
    foot.

I can describe my foot in detail,
The toes once pudgy now gnarled,
The toenails long and yellow and bent
Making permanent indentations on the nearby toes,
The peeling yellow mold that grows in between and under
The old and new scars,
And the old and new cuts from stomping my foot on the gray cold slats.

I can describe the slats in detail.
They are one inch thick by two inches wide
By however long the box is wide,
And they're tight against each other
So I can't see out
Except for where the steel-cutter slipped and left a space.
Their edges are rough, unfiled, newly cut steel,
And some of the screws stick up and are sharp,
And some of the edges are so sharp they cut.

It is a welcome pain when they cut me,
Wherever they cut me,
Because I can describe how that feels.
First, there's a jolt because I don't expect it.
Then, it sears for a minute and stings.
Then it turns into a dull ache
And, after a long time, it itches.

Later, it forms a scab, which eventually falls off.
I can describe that.
I can describe the box.
I can describe my foot.
I can describe the slats.

But I can't describe how I feel inside.
And I don't know how the box got INSIDE ME.

I realize that it is the frozen child who is speaking in this poem. Now, thirteen years after writing it, as I re-visit the poem in light of the words of the loving mother within, I know that that same child has begun to release some of those old feelings because she is safe enough to do so.

I thank all that is, Magdalen, divine mother, Yeshu, and the loving mother within, for teaching me how to allow and honor these feelings. I feel such warmth and tenderness for the child, and gratitude for her healing.

October 6, 2009

I went to my mother's house, my childhood home, for the last time yesterday.

I put my journal on the passenger seat, knowing I'd want to write. On the way home, as I drove, I wrote "Mama, Mama, Mama, Mama," the grief so loud. I felt frantic, like a hungry infant feeding and then abruptly torn from the breast midstream and thrown on a pile of offal, left to starve—little hands and feet splayed out and grasping at nothing but air, abandoned to her terror.

I ate some milk chocolate and felt a physical sensation of soothing move through me.

Still driving, I called my therapist. I couldn't answer her questions because I was too small—no words. When she explained that she was just talking to keep the connection, I felt a kinesthetic soothing similar to the chocolate, but it felt more enduring, as if I could keep the essence of it always, like the loving mother within.

It was the first time ever that human soothing went past my wall and in. At last, the starving, cold, wet, abandoned infant in the crib had a visceral experience of relief and peace. I feel the peace washing though me even now as I latch onto and re-live that remembered moment of human soothing.

How is it that I can feel Yeshu and Magdalen loving me, but it has been so difficult to allow human love in?

How, indeed?

12

TRANSMISSION OF LOVE

October 21, 2009

For the past few days, and especially this morning, I have felt this transmission coming in. In the chapter entitled "Loving Mother Within," the loving mother within explained and described the process of creating her, as well as her role and expectations. For this chapter, the masters are wanting a pure transmission of her infinite love imbued into her every word, as an activation for humanity and all universes. As I prepare, I am already deeply moved by the energy of what is coming.

Thank you, Beloveds. Thank you.

Loving mother within: *Dear one, beloved channel, beloved readers. The masters have asked for a transmission of love from the loving mother within, pure love coming in.*

I have called forth all of the ancient and archetypal lineage of loving mothers—from the stars, the trees, the winds, the caves, and tunnels, from every plane, level and dimension.

Magdalen is here. Mother Mary is here. The Lady Gaia is here. And I, the loving mother within, speak as a truly divine essence of loving mother loving you, each and every one of you. I enfold within me all of those who are here today, loving you, holding you, cherishing you in my embrace.

In each step that you take on your path, I love you. Each tear, each cry of anguish. Each shout of joy. I am here with you. There is no thing or action that could possibly be connected with you that I could not love. Every thought, every feeling, what you do, what you say, who you are in each moment of your life, I cherish as precious to me.

I am here, loving, holding, witnessing, and honoring you.

I, the loving mother within each and every one of you, am linked for all time with the ancient and archetypal Mother, the divine mother, the essence of the divine feminine. It is my divine purpose to be within you, a loving mother you can access if you wish, and I remain here loving you for all time.

I will not leave you. I will not turn from you. I will not judge you. This is my vow to you, dear ones.

Even in the times when you may turn from me, perhaps rejecting love because of the pain of even the thought of it, or because of past painful experiences of what was called love but was not. Even then, even when you turn from me, I remain, witnessing and honoring each step on your path.

Whether you live in an apartment, a house, a railroad car, under a bridge, in a mansion, in poverty, in wealth, alone or surrounded by friends and family, I am here, loving you, witnessing you, and honoring you.

When you look upon an orchid, I am that orchid, reflecting your beauty within, reflecting my love for you always.

There is no need or wish or desire too large, dear ones.

It is not my place to promise that your hopes and wishes and desires are all fulfilled in each moment. I am the divine feminine. I am not the one who acts. I am the one who loves, who holds, who embraces you, who witnesses, hears, honors every increment of your movement in this lifetime, on all planes, levels, and dimensions.

I have been with you in every lifetime, past, present, future, parallel, backwards and forwards to the divine plan of your soul.

I AM, in the same way of the I AM THAT I AM of the Great Love. I AM loving mother within each and every one of you.

No matter how small you may feel, in any moment, even if you feel unable to reach for me, I am here, hearing and witnessing your tears. I am here honoring your cries, your fears, your anguish, your despair, your need for solace.

I offer you that. I offer to you the anchoring knowledge of my being here with you, always, for all times, dear ones.

When all you know is the blinding fear and crying in the dark, even if you cannot grope your way to me, dear ones, I come to you and am here with you.

I love you.

I hold you.

I witness and honor you.

I am the crash and the ebb of the waves, the waxing and waning of the moon, the sliver of sunlight on your face.

My love is quiet. My love is gentle. My love has no expectations. You owe me nothing. I am simply here to love you and hold you, in my quiet way.

To me, dear ones, to those of us who are here—this ancient lineage of the divine feminine, the Mother Archetype, the ancient one, and also the unborn future all-and-timeless-one you are creating now within your soul—to us, you are precious beyond words.

Your every word, your every thought, your every feeling, your every action, is precious beyond words, each and every one of you.

My heart expands in love for you. My heart cries with love for you. As you fall asleep at night, I am there brushing back the hair from your brow, kissing you lightly, tucking you in, listening to your prayers, your fears, your thoughts, as you drift into sleep.

When your heart sings with joy, I am there, right there, right here, with you. When you feel absolutely alone, with nowhere to turn, I am right there, right here, with you.

Loving you—cherishing, hearing, witnessing and honoring you—this is my sole and divine purpose for all times.

I am threaded to the Hidden Source herself. I am threaded to the dark mystery of love that dwells there, that is the divine feminine.

I am the rich silence within that is filled with knowing, when you notice that something is right for you. When you cry the tears of truth, I am there with you, crying with you in gladness for your realization. In the moments of clarity, when the "ah-ha!" answer comes to you, I am sitting within you, smiling proudly, so glad, so glad for you.

Every moment, every breath, since the spark of light time and before, I have been here with you, always.

When you look in the mirror, I am looking through your eyes with you, and what I see is beautiful, always. Your size, your shape, your dimensions, I cherish, I devoutly honor.

How can I tell you how much I love you? How can I tell you how precious you are to me? There is not one other who is like you. You, each and every one of you, are special to the loving mother within you.

And when I see you create, when I see the magical child[G] within you burst alive and laughing and glad to be alive, I am joyous with you. I too am laughing aloud, with tears streaming down my face—your face!—with joy of you, delight in you and who you are and who you are becoming.

When you fall to the greatest despair, dear ones—each and every dear one, for I speak to each of you as precious—when you fall to despair, I am there kneeling down, grasping you in my arms and holding you, and stroking your hair, and letting you know that this too is a part of the path, a part of the lesson. And I tell you that you will move out of this despair and into the light of something new for you.

I weep in the moment of your falling into that despair, dear one. I cry for you, knowing how it hurts you, and how you wonder *if you will ever move out of that place. I am there in every fragment of your despair, right there with you, mourning with you the loss of your joy, or the seeming loss of yourself in that moment.*

And yet I also know that those moments when you fall into despair are a necessary part of the whole of who you are. For as you feel that despair, you are releasing it, that part of it, out of your cells for all time.

There is so much love for you here. The love is flooding from all the universes in this moment. It is as if you, dear one—each and every dear one—are the magnetic center of the ancient mother archetype love line, gathering all of the unconditional love of all true mother energies, vibrations, frequencies, from across all times, planes, and dimensions.

I am made up of Magdalen and Mother Mary and this planet—this beloved planet—the Lady Gaia, and the ancient tribal grandmothers who knew to sit together with you in the caves of the blood times, holding you, welcoming you into the family of the Mother.

And, dear ones, I speak not just to women here. I also speak to men. For were you not excluded from the red tent, the bleeding cave for women who bled or birthed their children? For you, there was no place to be held and allowed to grieve the loss of the feminine within you, the soft yielding place inside of you that longed for and was denied the permission to cry, to be held by your mother, to feel and express your feelings freely.

I speak to you, dear men, who hear this transmission of love. We include you here in our arms, precious ones. There is room for you here in our arms. For you also, dear ones, dear men, have a loving mother within.

Please know this. This is very important.

Of course, there is a loving father within, also. All who read these words, begin now to allow for the presence also of a loving father within, who comforts and holds you in a safe loving way. A loving father within who is strong and patient and acts as a loving teacher to you, to show you how to use the tools of your life's work. He does not judge you, nor does he demand or order you to do as he says. Rather he is a guide whose hand rests gently on your shoulder, giving you strength and courage and wisdom on your path.

Allow yourselves, dear ones, to begin to build his image too. As you walk the steps of your path, begin to notice those men around you whose attributes are loving and strong and wise, and draw from them the attributes of your own loving father within. Allow yourselves to lean into him to support you on your path. Know that this loving father within is gathered from the ancient and archetypal lineage of the divine masculine, which is embodied in Source itself.

With this transmission, we now connect you to that lineage, as well as the ancient and archetypal lineage of the divine feminine, the Hidden Source, that which loves in the silence and the mystery of all time, without judgment, without action.

We talk to all now, dear ones. I ask for you now, in this moment, to find a way to physically anchor—to remember in some way, in your body—this knowledge that the loving mother within is always present, always here within you.

Perhaps you may take the thumb and forefinger of one hand, and touch the tips of them together to create a circle and allow that circle to be a reminder of the love that I have for you, as I speak my words of love. So that even when you are in your pain and there are no words, and no way to reach out—no memory beyond the re-experiencing of the trauma in the little children— by placing your fingers thus, you can access the sensation of the Mother loving you, being with you, silently witnessing, allowing, and honoring your experience.

For those of you who do not know what I mean by a physical anchor, I will explain. When you put your hand in this position, your thumb and forefinger creating a circle—or perhaps your hand on your heart, or another way you choose—at the same time as hearing this transmission, this creates a physical memory in your cells that can link you to the knowledge of this transmission, of my existence here within you.

My existence within you, as a loving mother like the Goddess of Willendorf or Magdalen, or the Lady Mary, if you wish, or the Lady Gaia, this beautiful Planet Earth. Or perhaps I am a loving mother of your imagination, of your choosing, whatever feels right for you. Allow yourself to take a moment now and, if you can, and if it feels right for you in this moment, create for yourself an image of your loving mother within.

Or even ask that this image come to you, when it is the right time. Or ask that there be a team appointed, a light team, to create this image of the loving mother within for you, who may perhaps come to you in a dream or meditation. However you do this is exactly right, dear ones, each and every one of you, dear sweet children.

I ask that this transmission of pure love move through you, sweeping through and filling every atom, molecule, cell, and particle of your being with the light of this love, and the rich womb-warm darkness of love that I offer you. My divine purpose for all time is to love, hear, witness, and allow all that you are, to honor and cherish and see as precious all that you are.

And my wish for you, dear ones, is that you begin to know me. You begin to trust that I am here. You begin to count on my presence within you and begin to form an image of how I can love you and support you best. My wish is that you begin to live from this place for yourself, dear one.

I wish for you that the more you know me and trust my presence here within you, the more you will believe that I am here always, witnessing and honoring every increment of your process.

That you will begin to grow an ability that will become a habit of loving yourself as I love you. Of trusting yourself so that, even in the anguish, you know that you are loved. Even in the despair, I am you here loving you.

Dear ones, allow yourselves to be cradled within the infinite depths of love of the Hidden Source itself, the mother darkness, the divine feminine, in this silent beautiful gentle way. For that is the love with which I imbue you, that I offer you.

Precious, precious one—each and every one of you—precious, precious one, you are beloved of me.

I am this path that you are on.
Beloved. Precious one. Go in peace.
I love you.

I am more than filled. I am complete in this moment. All I can say is, *Thank you.*

PART TWO

Moving, Deconstruction

& Renovation

13

MOTHER OCEAN

February 11, 2010, Rockport, Massachusetts

I have moved many times in my life. When I left my husband in 1995, I drove a twenty-five-foot truck cross-country five times in three years, buying and selling three houses in three years, trying to find home. I moved, as a child with my parents, more than every year of my life until age six, and then again from the ages of fourteen to thirty-two, every year.

Ever since I moved to Massachusetts from California, there has been a longing inside me to live near the ocean again. In the years I lived there, the Pacific was "my mother and my father" and my soul place. When I left my husband, I moved east to be near my twin, leaving one heart for another.

On November 20, 2009, as part of my search for the Mother, I moved to the Atlantic Ocean.

I bought a tiny 600-square-foot house in Rockport, "as is," on the exact same little dirt road I had been exploring for ten years, wishing for a place of my own near the water. The previous owner had grown ill and died there, and the house was a wreck from top to bottom, all of her belongings still inside. It needed and still needs tender loving care.

I am finding that, as I heal this house, as I nurture it, I am also healing and nurturing my inner children.

It seems that ever since channeling the transmissions from the loving mother within, my inner children have felt freer to come out of hiding and exist in their true essence.

The ocean—the Mother—comforts and soothes me. From my little house on this dirt road, I can walk an hour and a half along a rocky coast to the end of a sandy beach and back. I can watch the sun rise over the ocean in the morning, and set over the ocean in the afternoon.

I have neighbors, a post office, bank, and library, all in my own town! I am no longer isolated, as I was in Leyden, the tiny rural town in Massachusetts where I began this book. I have already made four new friends.

The moon rises in my bedroom window in the winter. I hear crashing waves, wild winds, the foghorn, and train whistle and—now that spring is here—joyous birdsong throughout the day.

At times, I have felt I have abandoned Magdalen, Yeshu, and the masters, and even the great love of Source, but they have never abandoned me. I know that Magdalen especially is with me, as is the Mother.

They all, as I am, are watching and waiting, as I find my way.

I know that this little house is a gift from the Beloveds, a step on the path as my soul-self finds its way to freedom. A beautiful warmth spreads through my heart as it expands with love. I can feel Magdalen here with me, gently taking me into her arms.

Thank you, I say.

March 14, 2010

I came here to the ocean with the intention of writing.

But today, I see all the things that still need to be done and they distract me. I want to take care of them instead of writing.

Then I get a phone call from my neighbor saying the sandbags I put down are on his property, only three feet from my house. The wind is howling. The rain is beating on my windows. The room where I put my tiny desk is cold and sterile. It doesn't feel right for writing.

Where do I channel? Where in this little house do I begin to bring the Magdalene energy in? So far, no place here feels right. The house I left in Leyden had a 40' x 40' all-white room with vaulted ceilings where I channeled.

I give up for today and decide to play. This house has become a playhouse for me, and for all of the inner children. I have put little chandeliers in every room, and girly things, like pretty curtains and fringes and faeries. Crystals mark the perimeter with their sacred magic.

Every part of me wants to love it here. I don't know if I can. Again, I don't know if this is home yet. Maybe I'm just here to allow my inner children to explore and be and play.

April 29, 2010

I understand at last that "perfection" is a child's promise of Prince Charming and Happily Ever After, and I can accept that it is a faery tale. I had been looking for perfection in a home, in self, in my life.

I've moved things around and made them good enough. I've gone outside and sat in my little backyard and gone for a walk along the ocean, and I can feel the writing coming. I sit in the tiny guest room, my little white peeled-paint desk to the left of the window. I hear birds and the foghorn. I see the birches in the afternoon sun. I feel the peace and the stillness that awaits what is to come.

Again, I thank the Beloveds, the masters. I feel you here with me, as I feel my connection with myself—Beloved joining to beloved, in quiet joy. Has it truly begun again, at last?

14

ONCE UPON A TIME

April 29, 2010

All of my inner children are here with me, sitting on my lap and around me on the couch, with some of them on the floor beside me. They are clamoring for this story that comes from a magical place. I have put it in italics so that the voice of it is faraway and secret and hidden and safe. I write it for all of the inner children everywhere, in the hope that the love and the magic will embed itself into all who read it, only if you wish it.

Once upon a time, there was a tiny little girl who lived in a tiny little house, with a tiny little yard, on a tiny little road by the ocean. This tiny little girl was very very happy because living with her—in that tiny little house, with the tiny little yard, on the tiny little road by the ocean—were lots and lots of good, loving mommies.

There was a mommy who read her storybooks, holding the tiny little girl in her lap, brushing her lips softly and gently along the tiny girl's hair as she read, sometimes laughing, sometimes changing her voice to be the different people in the story, and sometimes leaning down and kissing her on the cheek and saying, I love you.

There was a mommy who brushed her hair very very gently and held it close to her head so that, when there were tangles, it didn't hurt her.

There was a mommy who tucked her in at night and sang her to sleep and kissed her goodnight and, when she was asleep, whispered loving words to her about who she was, and how she was loved, and how very very special and wonderful she was.

There was a mommy who made sure she got yummy tasty food, so she could flourish like a beautiful flower and have lots of energy to run and play and skip and jump and laugh!

There was a mommy who helped her understand her feelings, and named them for her when she didn't know what to call them so that she could know them, and her inside self, better.

There were mommies who tucked her in, and mommies who played with her, and mommies who held her when she cried and when she was scared. There were mommies who listened to every word she said, as if it was the most important thing to say in the whole wide world!

There were mommies who protected her from people who pretended to love her but who put her down any chance they got, and from people who lied to her, and from people who didn't care about other people at all but just about themselves.

The mommies would never, ever EVER let anything bad happen to her, and she knew it deep in her heart, and in her whole being, like a magic cloak wrapped all around her.

And probably best of all, all the mommies loved her exactly, absolutely, and positively, no-two-ways-about-it, JUST EXACTLY as she was.

The tiny little girl was very very happy because she knew that she was loved. She knew that she was safe. Because she had all of these good loving mommies, she wasn't afraid to ask for what she needed or wanted, and she wasn't afraid to say how she felt.

She knew who she was in a place deep inside of her that was special and secret, even from her mommies.

At that tiny little house on that tiny little road by the ocean, there were faeries in the tiny little backyard, and a baby dragon that slept with his tail hiding part of his eyes, but only part, so he could peek at people while he pretended to sleep.

The faeries lived in the flowers and flew around the little girl, and whispered and sang and laughed into her tiny little ears, and loved her too. She spoke to the faeries, and she could hear them talk back to her. She spoke with and played with the baby dragon too, for she had a magical imagination that made anything imaginary come to life and be real, and it was true.

Over time, the good loving mommies and the tiny little girl, with the help of the faeries and the baby dragon—who kind of helped but didn't really because he was mostly in the way but didn't know it— created a beautiful secret garden out of their imagination. When you went in the gate, you thought you were in a magical land that went on and on and on, even though it was just a tiny little yard.

Over time, other little girls came to play, girls who looked kind of like the tiny little girl but were different ages and had different memories, and different clothes and lengths of hair. The looks in their eyes were different too. When they first appeared, some of them were scared, or shy, or mute, or stayed to themselves. They appeared slowly, and then more and more bravely, as they learned that the secret garden was a safe enough place to be.

Again, over time, each little girl began to look at the others, curious, wondering, Why do they look like me? Who are they? How old are they? What are they thinking about? And then, lastly, one after another wondered, What does she know? What does she remember?

There would come then a rush of fear, a closing of the throat, a run to a hidden cave to huddle in a corner in the dark until the tiny little girl who was playing in the tiny little yard had a memory of another place and another time.

She realized that it hadn't always been like this, and that really all the other girls were different ages of the tiny little girl herself. She was especially glad now to be in the tiny little house on the tiny little road by the ocean, with all her good loving mommies around her.

She began to treat the other girls very gently, and to reach out her tiny little hands to them—pat, pat—and to love them, and listen to them, and tell them that it was going to be okay.

And slowly, the other little girls began to trust this place and trust the good loving mommies, and trust the tiny little girl and the secret garden place and the baby dragon and the faeries. Inside their little bodies, the jittery butterfly feelings slowed. One by one, they began to breathe a long long sigh, and then stillness and, finally, peace would come.

It had seemed such a long, long time that they had lived locked in terror of what they only remembered in tiny bits, in tiny locked-up places deep inside that kept them ever watching, ever wakeful, ever looking for the next scary thing to come. They could never sleep or rest or relax or do anything except hold those tiny locked-up bits, tight and hard, in those tiny locked-up places deep inside, because they didn't know what else to do with them.

They hadn't known about good loving mommies, or safe secret gardens, or tiny little houses with tiny little yards on tiny little roads by the ocean—or the possibility that they could be safe and loved and held and protected, as they were here.

Over time, Magdalen came to them, just as she had come to the tiny little girl who didn't remember her coming and thought she'd always been safe and loved and held and protected.

Over time, the other little girls felt safe and loved and held and protected too, as if they belonged for the very first time in their lives. They were no longer alone or afraid—well, only sometimes—but mostly there was so much goodness and love here, with the tiny little girl and all the good loving mommies, that they began to heal.

Magdalen didn't come as Magdalen. She came as the divine mother, as the mother darkness, as the loving mother within, but without those names, without those titles, without those faces. Rather, she came as a gentle infusion that grew deep inside the tiny little girl herself, that came from the good loving mommies all around her, in a house that was just her size.

This gentle infusion happened over months, without her even knowing it, as the tiny little girl—who, you see, was actually all the little girls in one and lived inside the body of a grown-up woman—worked on the tiny little house, cleaning it and painting it, and putting up faery princess chandeliers and sparkly light switches and lacey couch coverings and a pink crystal clock in the kitchen.

She placed pretty crystals all around the windowsills of the house too. In each loving addition she made to make the tiny little house hers, with her own magic and in her own delightful way, she brought more of this loving mother energy in.

Without realizing it, the tiny little girl inside the grown woman's body was following her unspoken instincts and infusing the tiny little house with the divine feminine and the mother darkness and the loving mother within, which became the good loving mommies to the tiny little girl, filling the tiny little house with the Mother's safety and protection and love, from her whole being.

And that tiny little girl and the good, loving mommies—and the other little girls inside—are all me, of course, but they can also be you, beloved readers, if you want them to be, for the magic infuses you here, now, if you wish it.

Just say the magic words: As you intend it, so does it happen.

This is a present for you, beloveds, all wrapped up in sparkly paper and ribbons and bows. It is a present for me too!

15

BATTLE OF THE VEILS

December 4, 2010, trailer in Colrain, Massachusetts

I have uprooted myself again and am beginning to feel desperate to find home.

As it turned out, my neighbors in Rockport didn't understand my need for privacy, my new friends had priorities that were different from mine, and the Atlantic Ocean was not a soul place ocean for me, after all. My time in Rockport did allow my inner children to begin anchoring the presence of the loving mother within, but I missed my twin and her little family here in Colrain, as well as my community of friends who are dedicated to the evolution of this planet.

So I have moved again, this time to a small mobile home, a trailer that I have fixed up and call "Le Petit Palais" because of the pink crystal chandelier I hung over the kitchen table!

This is again a stepping stone to my finding "true home" here in Colrain, a little town of 1,500 with a post office and gas station, farms, woods, intimate mountains, and people who remind me of the "old ways" of a time before I was born in this lifetime.

It has been since April that I last wrote for this book, and a year ago October since I last channeled for it. I have spent all this time getting the Rockport house ready to sell, and moving, and then fixing up this trailer.

I have not felt grounded for a long time. I am feeling terror about even attempting to channel again, wondering, will they have passed me by? They, the masters, Source? Will Magdalen have given up on me by now? Have I lost my right to speak, to write, to be one of the channels for this Magdalene energy—the divine feminine—for the collective consciousness?

Despite these questions, I have been seeing over the last few days, in my mind's eye, an image of myself as a twelve-year-old girl with long blond hair. Perhaps she is my magical child. She is my purity, my innocence, my light, my knowing that I am love. She is my right and my ability to speak the truth, to speak for the feminine, for the divine, for who I am, in all of my I-AM-ness.

As the twelve-year-old girl, I have a four-foot sword, and I see before me a thick swirling maelstrom of black clouds and, in the inky blackness, I see the faces and bodies of the demons of my fears and self-doubt. They have beaks for mouths, and big goblin ears, and they are leering and judging, jeering at me.

I am calling this channeling "The Battle of the Veils" because I know that the enormity of the absolute terror of this moment—of not being able to channel—is like a battle and is about more than just this moment.

There I am, the twelve-year-old girl with the four-foot sword, fighting the maelstrom of my demons. I live the feelings of this battle, as if it were real. It is the compounded experience of lifetimes, when I tried to speak the truth of the Source that I knew but backed down in the face of the jeering crowds who became my demons.

This lifetime is a time in which my soul is determined to ensoul, to be in this human body, speaking its truth through me.

I feel the tears in my heart, as I say this, because this book is about being on the path of the beloved, learning to treat myself as a beloved, transmitting the how of that through me, to bring to all. And I know that the path of the beloved is the path of the soul.

Part of the fear is around wondering, How can I transmit that information when I know so little about it? I know about love and I know about fear but can I trust that I can get out of my own way to allow the truth, the many truths, to come through me, in purity, and clarity, and love?

I have both hands raised, palms forward, and I can feel an immense heat and tingling of light and heat flowing through them. It feels as if this kinesthetic anchor helps me stay grounded right now as I channel my ensoulment.[G]

As I say that, I immediately feel fear, because what this battle is really about is the terror I sometimes feel when I even consider the possibility of taking up this sword, this transmission of the feminine, the beloved (whatever that means in its wholeness) in the face of my demons, the jeering crowds, my old doubts about myself and my abilities.

And yet, is it not wholeness that we are talking about in the end? The wholeness of bringing the divine feminine back to the planet, in its true power, and bringing the balance that comes with that?

I call it a battle of "veils" because I have felt the presence of an energetic veil—like a shimmering gossamer wall—just beyond the immensity of the battle that I see and feel in my entire being. It is as if beyond the veil is another land, a place of peace and beauty and stillness and safety.

The battle is one of many lifetimes, on many planes and dimensions, not just this one, and the feelings are compounded inside of me leading to a huge climax of terror. Perhaps, just maybe, I could pretend, right now in this moment, that I can physically step through that veil into the present and all those lifetimes aren't here.

Because really that's true! Those other lifetimes are not here in the present. The feelings are here, the terror and the physical sensations of being tortured, over and over—put to death, boiled in oil, hung, drawn and quartered, and more. What if I could see the present as just that, pure present, and allow myself to witness the feelings from a place of love, with the help of the loving mother within reminding myself that those lifetimes are not happening right now?

Yesterday, as I was going to the little guest room here in the trailer, to get my bag of tools—my headset, extension cord, external hard drive, my customary equipment for channeling this book (my truth)—the dread that was building up within me turned to terror. I knew it was that old terror of being put to death for speaking my truth.

Knowing all this, still feeling the terror, I said to myself, Let me pretend that I can step through the veil right into the present. I took a physical step across the imaginary line. I walked easily to the little guest room to get the bag. I said to myself, This is easy! I can't believe how easy this is! As I got closer, it was still easy. It was just an action of walking to get the bag.

When I came to within about five feet of the bag, I suddenly began to feel myself in a bleed-through experience[G] of crawling through a tunnel of whips, even though my physical body was still just taking one slow step at a time. Each whip had multiple steel-beaded thongs of leather. I was crawling through a tunnel of jeering people, each one whipping me.

I continued toward the bag, all the time feeling that tunnel of whips, the whips on my body, my skin torn, split, open, bleeding. I got the bag, walked back out of the room, and set the bag aside, still feeling lingering traces of the whipping. Still reeling from my experience, I wrote in my journal, aware of the immensity of what I had done.

Then, throughout the rest of the day, I felt the failure of not doing what I am doing right now (making this recording). Even though I had not planned on channeling, even though I had only planned on getting the tool bag to prepare for today, I felt the guilt of not channeling, a guilt not of this lifetime.

My guess is that some of you, my readers, may experience, at some times, feelings of extreme intensity, not knowing where they come from. I urge you to ask yourselves, Are these feelings about now? Can I step out of this context of other lifetimes, through the veil into the present, so that I can look at the feelings and begin to complete this unfinished business for my soul?

I was going to ask Magdalen to talk about resistance today, but I feel that we've already talked about it here. The resistance in my battle took the psychic form of a tunnel of beaded whips that "appeared" at the prospect of channeling my truth. So perhaps what I want from Magdalen today is just some words of validation, words of connection, words saying, Yes, she and the masters still want me to channel this book for them, for the divine feminine, for the Mother, for me.

So I call forth Magdalen now, with love, and I ask for her to let me know what she wants of me, at this time. And because it has been such a long time since I have channeled, I will begin by saying, *I am Magdalen*, as I was taught long ago in my first channeling class.

I feel tears in my heart because, immediately, I feel her coming through, and I feel such joy.

Magdalen: *Yes, dear one! Yes, of course we are here. Do you not know that we would never abandon you? Do you not all know—dear ones who read this book—that we would never abandon you?*

We sit here today listening to this one who had the courage to come forth and speak this truth today. We are taking a moment to collect ourselves. It has been a long time since we have channeled through this one, through her vocal cords, through her voice.

The message that we would say today is that we love you, each and every one of you.

I am having a difficult time feeling Magdalen here. I ask that I step out of my way. To strengthen the channel, I call forth the most beautiful channel of pure white crystalline light of the highest healing order, and I ask that the light of the masters come.

I open my eyes now and see the river out my window, and it is not Magdalen who wants to be here with me now. It is the Lady Gaia!

Lady Gaia, speaking for all the masters: *Dear one, how we love you! How glad we are that you have found this place! How glad we are to hold you in our bosom!*

How glad we are that you send your transmissions of love to this river, to these birds, to these great ones, the silent trees that have been here for so long, and that you have come home to yourself and, yes, we know you feel us now.

We are delighted that you are here in this moment, beginning again after such a long time.

Dear one, do you not know that you do not need a sword to fight the demons inside? You need only your heart that sings. You need only to remember that we are here always with you.

Yet we are pleased that you felt the battle within you, on all levels, that you moved right into the center of it, and re-experienced it for all lifetimes, consciously.

And, yes, the Tibetan (Djwhal Khul)^G is here smiling now. He is saying how you did indeed find a way to be playful, even in the moment of the battle.

You said, Let me pretend. As a small child might pretend there is magic, when indeed there is. You allowed the small child of yourself to pull the veil apart and tiptoe through to the other side, where the magic of this lifetime—the beauty of it—resides.

And, yes, dear one, we want you to continue this work. We want here, today, to simply connect with you, as you have asked, to remind you that we are here. Magdalen is here and loves you. She has not forgotten you.

There may be a shift in the transmissions now, for so much has changed within you in the last year. We too wish to continue this work, for it is of great importance to the collective consciousness of humanity and the intergalactic families,^G and we see the divine in you always.

And remember, as a dear friend said to you recently, "There is always a place in heaven for you, and there is nothing you can do to screw it up!"

We are laughing with you, joyously, in our reunion. And we feel that it is time for you to allow yourself simply to take in what you have done today, for you have broken through your barriers and come to us. Allow yourself now to just know that we are here, and that the rest of the book is coming.

With all of our love, with our gratitude and our blessings, dear one, we leave you now.

Go in peace.

Goodbye for now.

Thank you, Beloveds, I say. *I am so relieved. It has been such a long time. How easily I forget sometimes who I truly am.*

Thank you.

16

VISITATION

December 8, 2010

The book I was reading last night listed a number of flowers, one of which was a tulip. I found myself immediately in Yeshu's "The Teen and the Tulip" chapter,[9] which talks about the natural timing of the tulip, of all plants and all beings.

Suddenly, standing there in the tiny aisle between the side of my bed and the exterior wall, was Yeshu just a few feet from where I lay. Magdalen then "appeared" at my left, standing "through" the bed. They were both reaching towards me, with love and compassion.

I began to weep with the relief of this reunion. I was so glad to what I call "see/sense" them again. I *knew* they had come to tell me they loved me and wanted me to continue with this book. I *knew* I would journal what they wanted to say in the morning, but right now I wanted to keep reading because I was almost finished with the book.

This morning, in the magic time between darkness and dawn, my heart is full of love, joy… and fear. How can that be? I can *feel* my resistance, even in this moment, to contacting them and journaling what they want to say to me, and yet I do it.

Sweet ones, I begin, *what did you want to tell me last night?*

Yeshu: *Dear one, although it has been such a long time, do not fear your purpose here. Do not fear your heart's desire. We are here. We are right here.*

It matters not what the circumstances or surroundings are. We will not let you down. It is only you who can seem to let yourself down, dear one, even when you don't. Remember the timing of the tulip. Open your heart to me. Feel my hand touch yours. Feel my hand touch your cheek, as it does.

Feel Magdalen here, and the others.

See them standing in this room.

Yes, we see now. You feel us as judges of the Inquisition, testing you. Dear one, you know that this is a bleed-through experience. You know that this feeling is not us.

We hear your silent cries: It is the room! The small size of the room! But you and we both know that "it" is not that. Magdalen comes now. Allow her to speak, knowing we are all here for you.

I say, *Magdalen, I can't see or feel you clearly because the webs and sludge of all this moving from house to house makes my* connection murky. *How can I let you through, trust you if I can't trust myself?*

Magdalen: *Sweet Leslie. Sweet one who I call Leslie in this lifetime, who has been a sister, a friend, a beloved to me in many, many lifetimes.*

I answer: *Magdalen, I can hear you but when I go to channel you in the recordings, it feels as if a gate slams shut.*

Magdalen: *It is your fear shutting the gate, dear one. This is your persecution overlay. Remember what that beloved friend of yours said to you not many weeks ago.*

Say it now: I am peace. I am light. I am love.

Feel it calm you. Feel the peace move through you. That peace is me speaking through you. That peace is you speaking through me. That is the unspoken Mother.

You are feeling the fear of those lifetimes of the Inquisition in all its many forms, in so many planes and dimensions. You continue to release those lifetimes as you began, a few days ago, as you have written. But dear one, even stronger than that fear and even more enduring is your own light. Let your light shine like a beacon into every nook and corner of your darkness. Allow your light to shine.

Notice how you have been looking for me outside of you, and here I am inside of you, in your fingers, in your pen, in your very knowing, in the place of the divine feminine deep within you.

You have worried that you know nothing, or not enough, about the divine feminine. Of course, dear one, for the feminine, the Mother is not known! She is felt. She is a knowing, a sense, an inner strength, but she is not a "known," as can be memorized, and learned by rote, and recited. Let that knowing speak through you.

The Inquisitors over lifetimes wanted names, dates, facts. They wanted to trap and capture that which could be touched. But they could never capture or put to death the knowing, for that is untouchable. What you have, who you are, that which is light, love, peace, knowing—none of that can be cornered, tortured, held fast, or put to death.

Is this not so, dear one? Is this not so?

We are glad you feel this anguish. For it is the pressure of your soul to know and to speak the truth at last, is it not?

Remember, dear one, that even as you have been looking to feel me outside of you, I am here inside of you, right here in the bridge chakra^G between your heart and solar plexus, right in this moment!

I know you can also feel me outside of you too now, cupping your face with my hand. Yes, that is me, dear one.

Remember, you are peace. You are light. You are love.

Let these words be the way to open the door to me, and also to your self, to your ensouled self.

Go in peace now, dear one.

Go in peace.

Thank you, Magdalen, I say.
Thank you, Yeshu.
Thank you, Beloveds.

17

CASTLE IN THE MISTS

January 18, 2011, Colrain, Massachusetts

The masters have found me my next place, a temple, a castle in the mists right here in the mountains of Colrain. It is a place to fulfill my soul's promise of channeling, writing, and finding a home for my soul at last.

I see them, masters on the etheric plane, lounging on luxurious couches in the greatroom with its fifteen-foot-high riverstone fireplace, cathedral ceiling, and views of the Catamounts, the black ledge hillside, and a waterfall across the valley.

They are initiating, strengthening, activating, and preparing the castle, as well as the channel that connects the heavens through the granite ledge here to the crystalline center of this beloved planet. I have seen them laughing, talking, taking out their akashic^G appointment books—lifetimes ago—and penciling in this month as the time that my soul will occupy this healing sanctuary, to root at last, or so I hope.

Backing up to the thirty acres of woods that will be called "mine" are hundreds of acres of Audubon land and forest preserve. I am blessed beyond all my expectations.

There has been much internal change. "The book" is coming closer and closer in my psyche. My dreams are pointing the way to the renewed and strengthened magic of my soul's life in body.

I have felt an extreme agitation at times, that I now recognize as my soul's anticipation and expectancy of finally living my soul's purpose, in every facet of my life. I struggle with the idea of making a commitment to that purpose because the idea of commitment has always provoked images of persecution and torture, if I fail.

Now, however, each obstacle standing in the way of closing on this beautiful place has been easily overcome once I adopted an expectation of ease, knowing that the masters would not abandon me, after their having found this place for me.

I find myself buying crystals to further the current of the channel that flows down right through the riverstone chimney, a huge white quartz crystal at its heart. I know now that the other houses were all part of my path, my unfolding, and self-discovery. I visit this house daily until it is mine, loving it, marveling in tears that it will soon be mine.

For so long now, I have known that, in countless past lives, I was a queen, a ruler, a chieftain, all put to death by the mobs. I had always thought that my deaths were caused by my actions and decisions that came from my love of and advocacy for the people.

Just recently, I learned the truth through a piece of regression work.

I am the seven-year-old eldest son of a Native American chieftain. I love nature, the animals, birds, flowers, the river—the blessed ripple of water as it reflects the sky—the breeze blowing through the leaves.

I am swimming naked in the river, my breechclout on the bank. I gently cup a fish in the palms of my hands, and stroke it and whisper to it, knowing its thoughts, its dreams, its being. I lie on my back and float, lost in the peace of the overhanging branches. I hear the birds calling each other. A doe drinks peacefully at the river's edge.

Suddenly, a shot rings out. It is a white man's rifle from across the river. I hear the jeering and laughter of the hunter and his friends. I see them clap each other on the back and then walk away.

The doe looks up at me, startled, and then falters and falls to her knees. I cry out, seeing her, and I swiftly swim to the shore and kneel, sitting on my feet, and take her head in my lap, stroking her. Her big brown eyes look into mine, questioning what has just happened, and then she dies in my arms.

My heart slams shut.

I have known that my people hunt for food but I have not been present at the killings. I have helped to dress the animals and I have eaten them, but my people have never left the animal to die and rot, without taking it with prayers of gratitude for its sacrifice.

Because of my love for the planet and all beings of nature, I form a thought that changes my entire existence and, later, that of my tribe: I decide all white men are evil and must be killed.

I am now the old chieftain, sitting cross-legged, with my last surviving son lying dead across my legs. I am the sole survivor of my tribe. I have spent my life blindly leading my warriors to hunt and kill all whites, despite the pleas of my people who are eventually all slaughtered.

The dam of my heart breaks open. I finally feel the grief, long held in check, for my family and people, all dead, because of me, because of that one conclusion I made as a child.

I now realize, too late, what I have done.

The tears roll down my wrinkled, leathered cheeks.

I am alone.

Here, now, looking at that lifetime, and at the same time, being the chieftain, I heal this heart.

I realize that in that lifetime that exemplifies so many, I did not listen to the people. I hear, *Is listening not one of the aspects of the Mother? Is this not one of the aspects of going within, into the mystery, into the unknown, into the place of allowing the inner and outer voices to speak, including the voices of the people?*

Is this not the aspect of getting out of one's way, to just be and allow that which unfolds, knowing that there is no right, no wrong, but only the connection of the heart to all that is? A connection that creates an action formed from connection, rather than isolation? Hear this, dear ones (speaking to all). *Know this, dear ones.*

I realize that it is not important if this is the house where I am meant to live for the rest of my life. What is important is that I listen to all aspects of myself, in connection with my heart.

I now release that unlistening aspect of myself and, with it, all the lifetimes of that aspect so that I can at last be free. I am stunned with this new realization, stunned and grateful.

Over many lifetimes, my soul built up a habit of being punished for actions that I, in my solitary place at the top, as the "committed" ruler, believed I was doing for the good of the people. As a result of this expectation of punishment, I have often felt a lethargy, a resistance, even a kind of apathy, towards making any commitment at all, even to do what is my soul's purpose. I understand this now.

Even with this house, this castle in the mists, I have doubted myself, my ability to make the "right" decision about where I am meant to live, after so many moves. What came to me a few days ago was the question, If I commit to this house, does that then mean that I commit to myself?"

And then I asked myself, What if I just decide to stay? My answer is: Well.... And then, okay.

Could it really be that easy? Is it really true that once the decision is made, all else follows?

I imagine etheric pages reshuffling themselves and restacking on top of each other, creating a new order of things. The real commitment though is simply to commit to myself with love, whether or not I stay in this house. It is about staying with myself, staying with this path of learning how to treat myself as a beloved.

January 16, 2011

I realize that my inner children have been panicking about this next move, so I spend some time with them, listening to their fears, speaking with them and comforting them. Who could blame them? Then, I call on the Tibetan to give me healing, and all the masters come in, as one, soon after.

All will be well, they say.

I close my eyes and allow the healing to happen. Immediately, I feel my heart radiating rippling waves of warmth.

They continue: *Every step of the way, we are with you. The agitation you feel is the agitation of your soul on the brink of its fulfillment. This is where you belong at this time, dear one. Every step of the way, we will be with you, and every step is sacred.*

Know that we are here with you, even now, preparing the way. The crystals you are buying are tools of your initiation, and the tools of the initiation of the Castle itself.

Bring the children. There is always a place for them. Remember them. Listen to and allow their feelings. And listen to and allow us to speak to you and be with you in this unfolding. Feel the children here right now, as we speak to you all.

Know yourself. Recognize your holiness and your humanness, for both are sacred.

Yes! Start a bell choir, as you have been wanting to do! Play and do the work of the masters, for is this not one and the same? To live fully—loving, playing, rooting, connecting—is this not the "work" of the masters?

Again, this agitation is simply your soul eager to come to rest at last, in the place where it belongs for now.

Do not make this move just about work! Allow yourself to play, even in the work! Your ensoulment and your playing are equally important, even one and the same. Allow them to be equal parts of your commitment too, bringing it to a place of light and joy, dear one!

PART THREE

Magic Returns

18

KEEPER OF THE LAND

February 2, 2011, Castle in the Mists, Colrain, Massachusetts

It is long long ago, in the time when the planet is first forming. Her fires are breathing her into form and creating mountains, seas, the great ledges, and continents.

As the waters recede, in the land where the sun rises, a mountain range forms, undulating softly, reaching out to stretch towards the light. From one of its peaks, it creates for itself—out of its ethers, from the very center of the earth—an invisible keeper who is born of love and silence, mystery and enchantment.

This keeper carries the voice of the mountain, breathes it, sings lullabies to it, and cares for it, as plants and trees, mosses and flowers begin, over time, to surge up from the heart of the mountain to its surface.

She, the keeper, becomes the soul of the mountain itself.

This keeper, invisible to the human eye, feels like a crone, a wise woman, arms held out to love the now-ancient stone, the ledge, the oak trees hundreds of years old, the woods alive with faeries, deer, woodchuck, fox, coyote, and birds of all colors, shapes, and sizes.

The keeper watches and waits as humans first appear.

She looks out across the long-formed valley to the mountains, and waits patiently while natives come and go, honoring her mountain, loving her, worshipping and adorning her. She waits patiently while the natives are hunted by each other, and then by the white man, and then are no longer.

She waits silently, while white men come to score her ledge, dig into her breast and sides, and build a structure (a dwelling place) of wood, concrete, tar, and asphalt. She waits until these too are gone, knowing that there will some day be one—as she knew so long ago when she was first born of the mountain—who will listen, love, cherish, know, and understand without being told, the truths, the knowledge of all that has gone before, and all that will come.

The structure empty, the ascended masters come and take up residence. They wave their wands and speak their incantations and initiations, and laugh and lounge and play, in preparation. On the etheric planes, they create a castle of crystal and stone out of a structure of wood.

Merlin comes, flies in, flies out, bringing a baby dragon with him to breathe fire and the magic of new beginnings into the place.

Yeshu comes. Magdalen comes. They make etheric love in front of the hearth, creating fire in the stones.

Vywamus in his formlessness comes to strengthen the channel that is already there.

The faeries come, flitting right through the windows into the castle, and sprinkling magic dust on its walls and floors and ceilings, to protect it from the humdrum of the everyday world.

All is in readiness.

The door opens.

And she-who-has-been-awaited appears on the threshold, with tears of joy and delight running down her cheeks.

She takes her place in the magic.

And time begins, ends, then no longer exists.

Such is the magic that resides here.

19

HONORING THE SELF

February 2, 2011

I love the previous chapter, for the magic that stirs there. And I know that even when I don't feel the magic of this path of ensouling and learning to love myself, there is always an undercurrent of magic in all that I do.

What amazing beings humans are! I am often astounded and in complete awe of how utterly complex we are, especially when we are attempting to know and heal our souls and move to the place of treating ourselves as beloved.

The day before yesterday, I sent an email to a friend, basically ending our relationship because I was not willing to give of myself as much as she seemed to want of me. I needed more time to be, to write, to ensoul and that does not leave a lot of time for relationships that don't really work for me.

The friends I keep are the ones who understand this and who are also committed to their own paths of ensoulment and learning to love themselves. It is a joy to spend time with them and that time feeds my soul.

For months, I had felt anger and guilt because I'd wanted to end it but didn't know how. I spent hours deliberating over the email, writing and rewriting, trying to make it perfect, kind, compassionate, until I ended up not saying what was really true for me, to save her feelings. In the end, her feelings were hurt anyway and would have been, no matter what I said.

That night after sending the email, I felt so much guilt that I woke up with an intense headache. I wondered why I couldn't just let it go. I knew this was a huge soul piece for me. I knew it involved past lives and karma. So, I asked the masters.

The masters respond: *Dear one, above all, know that you are loved. Know that all that you do is in the name of love, and that love commands your life. Your compassion is strong. Lean on it. Allow it. Do not fight it. It is a great strength.*

But also, dear one, have compassion for yourself. You are struggling and searching to find the way to live in honor of yourself, and to put aside the old ways of service. For many lifetimes, you were in service to others in one way or another, for the greater good—for the people, the tribe, the country, the planet.

It is now time, in this lifetime, to honor and serve yourself before all others. In this way you become a shining light to others, for humanity. Until you shed the robes of service, you cannot take on the garments of mastery which is in itself a higher form of service but one of freedom in service. Allow this.

We understand your confusion, for just recently, you have explored the lifetimes in which you wrongly assumed you were acting on behalf of the people, for which you were punished. But, dear one, do you not know that you are also embedded with lifetimes of protecting the people, too? Caring for them, living for them, dying for them?

And now, suddenly, you are given—or rather you are taking and claiming—this lifetime for yourself, here in this castle, in the name of honoring yourself, your true self.

And, yes, we too see the many who have fallen, slaughtered by the warrior that you were in some lifetimes. We feel you pulled down by your compassion for others. It is no longer the time for self-flagellation. It is the time to love yourself deeply, in your earnest efforts to come to mastery.

For reasons clouded by lifetimes, you were not able to allow your light to shine with this friend. You could not be who you truly are with her.

Allow the details not to be known, or understood. Simply allow that you have chosen to free yourself of more than this relationship. You are freeing yourself from the forces of intolerance and judgment that have held you back from your path for lifetimes.

Remember that love is saying "no" to that which does not feed you or feel right for you. Your divine knowledge has spoken. Do not punish it with self-flagellation on behalf of others. Applaud it. Welcome it. Know that what you have done is absolutely right for you. There is nothing else you could have done except for kneeling before the chopping block, for is this not how strongly you feel it when your soul is at risk of enduring yet another lifetime lived without attaining ensoulment?

Allow the divine feminine, the mother darkness, her mystery. Allow that this does not have to be clear. Allow that you have found the path even in your blindness. And the path is one of honoring the self above all others. We know you do that with all integrity—beyond all integrity, dear one!

So, love yourself, delightful one, as we do!

You have done no wrong. Allow the loving mother within to comfort you in this. Remember that she is always available to you, as we are.

Yes. Thank you, I say.

I feel so much better with the reminder just to love this part that feels the guilt. Love floods through me and I sigh with relief.

20

NOTHING TO FORGIVE

October 21, 2011

It is ten months later. This present house, the one I call my castle, needed much more physical work than any of the others, despite the fact that the masters were preparing it for me on the etheric planes before I moved in.

As I write this, I am thinking how, in this house, my soul has begun to come into my physical body, ensouling. I needed that ten months to renovate the house and for time to myself, to get to know the land here and who I am becoming. I know that much has been happening subliminally, and I was not yet clear enough nor ready to share with my readers. It is time now to "take up the pen" and continue.

Something that I have been thinking about a lot is the idea of free will. We humans have free will, but what makes us use it to our benefit? What makes us decide to move out of lethargy when we feel it, decide that we want to move forward?

This morning after two solid days of workmen here, I went to the waterfall. I felt such relief and gladness to be there, and yet, nagging and lurking and lingering under that gladness was a visceral weight of feeling, an ancient hard stuckness, embedded in the stone at my center, and my gladness was like the falls spilling and washing over the stone.

I allowed myself to surrender to this visceral weight of feeling, and waves of old shame began to pour out of me. I placed myself in the center of the circle of masters, and I allowed myself to receive their love, and yet somehow, the feelings seemed endless, and their love was not enough, only temporary.

How can I do this for myself? I asked. How can I be a part of this so the healing becomes permanent? How can I clear this old energy out of my physical, emotional, and causal^G bodies, for good?

I stepped into my master role and joined with the other masters in sending wave after wave of love into the "I" that felt so much shame and I allowed the love in at the same time. Still, the love was not enough. The masters' love was not enough.

I allowed my shame self to let those feelings rise and release, and still there was so much more. I told myself, I am worthy. No response came from the shame self. It felt like a bandaid phrase. And finally, I heard, *There is nothing to forgive.*

It was the circle of masters whispering in my ear, surrounding me with their love, and saying, *There is nothing to forgive.*

The tears began to course down my cheeks. The old hard place of the shame of lifetimes began to soften and melt away, as if it were part of that waterfall.

I began to repeat this to myself: *There is nothing to forgive. There is nothing to forgive.*

And I realized the truth of this. That no matter who I am or what I do, I am loved always. There *is* nothing to forgive. All that I do is part of the path. All that I am is part of the path. And my devotion to the path speaks for itself.

(Even in this moment, much later, editing, the peace and the healing of this washes through me.)

It was as if that sentence, as spoken in the circle of healing for the part of me that feels shame, had activated a pathway of release and transmutation, a gateway through which the heaviness could travel and disperse. My gratitude knew no bounds.

As I repeated this phrase to myself, I felt the masters all around me, standing in the woods, on the cliff by my side, walking and contemplating amongst the trees, supporting me. With the release of the shame, my magical child began to be curious. I began to wonder about the physicality of emotion in the fifth dimension.[G]

Is there still this quality of physicality in multidimensionality? If not, I would miss the expansion of my heart in joy, and even the compression of my heart in pain, as I had felt it today. I would miss the physicality of my self. I looked down from my great rocks and again "saw" the masters walking among the autumn leaves, by the stream that moves through the trees below the waterfall. How could the earth and her beings lose their physicality, when she is so much a part of the masters' experience? Is not physicality a part of the multidimensional experience also, if it includes all dimensions? I heard, *Yes, of course!*

I was gladdened and delighted, thanking the falls, the masters, the angelics, devas, faeries, and elementals. I left the falls to walk down the mountain to journal what I had learned, at peace within myself, with the belief that there is nothing to forgive.

Perhaps that was the piece that was missing for me, that I was asking about, around free will. Even in a state of lethargy, what if I decide to picture myself in the center of that circle of masters, as the part who feels shame or lethargy—or whatever else shows up in the moment—and repeat to myself, as the masters said, *There is nothing to forgive?*

It seems that the moment I do that, the lethargy dissipates. It is no longer just up to me alone to move forward. I have support and love along the way.

There is much to learn. I will continue to experiment.

Beloveds, thank you.

October 25, 2011

I have been thinking about all of the inner and outer children who have been told, through looks, words, or punishments, that they must forgive someone who hurt them. I speak here as to a young child.

I ask that whatever part of you can understand these words, please pass them on, in a way that can be understood by the littlest ones who either have yet no words, or are not old enough to understand these words.

I want to tell you now that you don't ever have to forgive anyone unless you want to. I am not in any way saying that it is okay for bad things to happen to you. That is not something that any one of the ascended masters who love you, would want for you.

The love that comes from the masters in the circle is like magic that heals lots of things, and it can also heal that place inside that feels scared and confused when someone asks you to forgive someone who hurt you. Forgiving is not a child's job, and never has been! If grown-ups want to forgive someone who hurt them, that is a different thing.

Also, if you feel you have been bad, please know that that could never be true. Sometimes, we all do things that we wish we hadn't done, things that some people might call "bad," but that does not mean that we are bad. When you feel that way, the loving masters want to tell you that there is nothing that you did that needs to be forgiven.

You are loved for exactly who you are, always. Magdalen and Lady Gaia, and the loving mother within, love you and there is never anything you could ever do that would take their love away.

It is okay to just let the magic of the masters' love come to you, and only if you want it, dear little ones.

Just wish for it, or you can pretend you have a magic wand and wish for it, and it will come, the way magic does!

21

MY MOTHER'S MOTHER'S MOTHER

December 15, 2011

I just finished unpacking, for the first time since 1995, a small white paper sculpture I did when I first moved to Massachusetts from California. It is called "My Mother's Mother's Mother."

It is twists of medium-weight white paper forming an infant, lying in the lap of a little girl with a pigtail, who is curled in the lap of a mother sitting in the pose of Michaelangelo's Madonna in his sculpture "The Pieta."[10]

As I unpacked it today, I began to wonder about the first human mother. I mused to myself: If only that first mother had listened deeply, noticed, and allowed—and had known without words or thoughts or sensations—that she was held in the all-accepting, all-encompassing love of the mother darkness, the Mother who is known and not known.

And if only, in recognizing that pervasive love and acceptance, she had then become imprinted with that knowing, and created within herself a loving mother, with the ability and facility for those qualities of nurturing. If only she had then passed that imprint down through the ancient and archetypal lineage of all time, to the present.

How, then, would we be different?

If we had known from our embryo's inception that we were not only held in the physical womb of our birth mother's body, but also deeply embedded and cradled within the many-times-more-powerful and magical, transmutational womb of the Mother herself.

What if we knew this in our whole beings, and lived from within that knowledge in every breath, act, moment of our lives?

And the fathers too. Being imprinted with this knowing in the womb, before gender development, long before birth. Replacing the anguish over the separation from the physical mother and, therefore, unconsciously, the separation from his own feminine self. Replacing that anguish with the all-pervasive knowledge that the Mother's love is imprinted within him.

How would our lives, our reality, be different?

I wonder.

22

UNDER THE ANCIENT ONE

December 20, 2011

I sit on leaf-carpeted earth and lean back against an ancient maple tree, a "great one" that is four feet across, and I know that it continues to grow and listen and watch.

Beneath me, under the surface, I feel the presence of the being I met in a dream once, who lives inside the earth itself. He too leans against the great one but deep beneath the earth's surface, against its great roots. He is listening, with every sense, to she-who-walks-the-land above.

I feel his thoughts, as if he is sending them to me, through the roots. I "hear" him saying, *I feel her heart, her uncertainty, her light, as it shines down the root system to my back. She waits in the stillness of the trickling of the nearby brook, the muted rush of the far stream. She waits till the stillness surrounds and envelops her and reminds her that she is home.*

I wait too, silently, reaching my force field up through the roots, up through the sap—the blood of the ancient one—in an effort to send her, with the great one's love, my own love and support. She has been alone in remembering us. I would thank her and ask her to tell our story.

There is no need for her to hurry. The brook, the stream, these sap-filled veins, this ancient one—none hurry. They live as they live. Their living, their being, is end in itself. There is nothing more the brook, the stream, or the ancient one need for their adornment. They are all that they are. They are the I AM THAT I AM.[G]

Somehow, she tries over and over to create this effortless perfection, this peace and stillness and beauty, in her home, in herself. I hope that she may come to know that what she searches for is the Mother, the mother within. In the deeply embedded feminine inside of her, she does know it. Yet the masculine within searches endlessly through doing, in efforts to create the feeling of this peace.

I have sat beneath this great one's roots for long periods of timeless darkness, and let the knowledge seep into me, as the underground springs seep into the earth. No one can tell her. No one can show her. Only she can find this for herself. Only she. She continues to search outside of herself for that which she already has inside.

I hope that she will come to notice the moment when she stops at the gate within her, just before entering. I hope that she will explore the story, the essence and make-up of the gate so that some day, at last, she can go in. Yet I know that, in her searching and telling of her search, she tells the story of the unfolding of many. Perhaps she is like a walking lighthouse with her story. Perhaps.

I go now to join my mate, and to hold her and silently impart to her my compassion for this one who searches. We who live in these caves and roots and hollows and darkness under the earth, we know where we belong.

And yet I see, through the dark silence here, that every stroke of her adornment of house is indeed adornment of self, another step towards creating and knowing herself. The act of the adornment allows her to listen within and respond to that whim of creativity. In creating without, she creates within.

For her, the process of the adorning is in itself a way for her to explore who she is. Like a dance, the house, the different rooms, even her different past houses, lead and she follows, and vice versa, as she listens and responds to the subtle nuances of taste and inspiration within her: naming what she likes and dislikes, what calls to her and what does not. The process offers an unbounded delight and joy in the visual and sensual unfolding of who she is becoming.

For her, when the act is complete, it is not so much that she is pleased but that she feels herself more complete, more at peace.

We have no need of this creating, for we are already complete within the home of the mother darkness.

Beloved Mother, beloved darkness, please send your love spiraling through the blood of these roots to she-who-walks-the-land, in the hopes that she may know your peace within herself some day.

23

IMPATIENCE OF A MASTER

January 4, 2012

I take a moment now just to center myself, in this force field, these trees, these mountains, for is not the multidimensional realm, the realm of all of these at once, and much much more?

This past weekend was New Year's Eve weekend 2011, going into 2012. I took part in a three-day intensive workshop at the School of the Golden Discs[11] here in Colrain, around the topic of multidimensional consciousness.

I went in on Friday excited about the workshop, eager to join with others who feel as I do about humanity and the planet's evolution. I continued to be excited until, after lunch, the Tibetan spoke to us, through Moriah Marston[12] who channels him.

I soon found myself extremely irritated and impatient because the material felt redundant and slow to me. I became depressed and disappointed in myself, as everyone oohed and aahed with awe after the channeling. I felt impatient and angry at myself for not having been able to take in what the Tibetan was saying, and I could not understand this.

The rest of the day I had a difficult time focusing and attending. I tried to move out of my impatience and irritation with myself and the material and with the pace of humanity's progress into multidimensional consciousness—the human pace toward understanding and moving into that place.

I mentioned my irritation and upset to Moriah at the end of the day, in tears of disappointment. She said that the impatience goes much further than this lifetime, for I have been a master in many lifetimes. I lived with them for many lifetimes, and this issue is related to that time.

The next morning, New Year's Eve morning, I was still in angst about this impatience and about my inability to take in the words of this ascended master, the Tibetan. I realized I needed to get up early and work with myself, speak with the masters and share with them and my own master self, what was going on.

I have not been channeling ascended masters recently. I have not been called to do so because I have been called to channel my own master self (my highest soul self). I have begun to trust this self, my own inner knowing, for I know that it comes from that Hidden Source within me.

The following is what came to me New Year's Eve morning in a discourse with the masters. I have attempted to imbue these words with the level of energy that I felt as it came through, as I feel it now.

I ring chimes to begin the transcribing and, as I do this, I notice that the frequency of the chimes recreates and returns me to the feeling of the multidimensional realm. So begins my effort to find clarity and understanding of myself, and also of the masters' timing, the divine timing, in bringing this multidimensional consciousness to humanity.

I ask, *Sweet Ones, will you help me please?*

The masters answer, *Look into yourself, dear one. We feel your grief and your tears.*

The Tibetan asks, *Is it really that you don't want to hear me speak?*

And I answer, *Yes. What you say asks too much from me! It forces me to the altar!*

I remember a past life where priests are dragging me, struggling, to the altar, and one of them—tall, forbidding, and stern—says, Now, you must listen, and you must vow to repent, and accept these words and this way!

I try to stop my ears with my hands, once they have released me there on the cold stone floor. But they tear my hands away, and I am made to kneel there, my face forced up to face the stern one, tears rolling down my cheeks, and I am defeated.

I know there is more: I feel myself in the circle of masters, and I am the willful one, the oddball, in that lifetime. I speak out and say, *ALL should know this multidimensional consciousness, and what it is, now!*

They answer, *It is not the time. Humanity is not ready.*

And I say, speaking to the masters now, *Now IS the time!*

And they answer, *Yes, now, you are ready to begin.*

I can feel my anger and the strength and depth of my emotion in this moment. The masters are here, and they watch, and they talk and talk, and they allow humans to make their way, ignorant and erring, without interference, albeit with love and support.

Why did we have to wait two thousand years for this "new" consciousness when it was known then? I rail. *Why did we have to struggle, we humans, through the dark ages, the plague, all the wars, famine and suffering? Why did humanity have to go through all that, when it was known then, two thousand years ago?*

For I remember, in my body in this moment, all the words of Yeshu then, all of his knowledge, all that he knew when he came to embody the Great Love, which is Source.

I knew that the masters knew two thousand years ago in linear time all that they know now. *So,* I say to the masters, continuing to rail at them, *Why couldn't you have helped show the way, long before this time now? I understand that survival was most important, for centuries, but what of the kings, queens, and nobility, the merchants and knights? Why couldn't you get through to them? Why only now?*

I am impatient with the slowness of the human process—of noticing and loving the parts, the emotions, the issues that we humans would rather disown—rather than the masters offering the healing that could be effortless and immediate, so that all can leap forward to access their multidimensionality.

Why have humans had to struggle, like toddlers, learning over and over how to walk, for centuries, for eons?

I am given the image of a 2000-year-old oak. One life. Two thousand years. Barely perceptible movement. Its roots slowly growing deeper into the earth, its leaves reaching to the sky, swaying in the wind, harboring squirrels and birds, budding in its branches, wisdom in its very sap. Two thousand years is but the snap of a finger in the multidimensional realm.

The laborious process of taking the time to love the parts that we would rather deny seems slowest of all, to the master self and the human self at this time. Maybe I just don't want to feel! says the human self. Maybe I just don't want to love myself, or nurture myself, because it hurts. It brings up so much pain.

And I feel the circle of masters, in this moment, surrounding the "so much pain," seeing the colors of that "so much pain," noticing, observing, having compassion for that which is "so much pain," and showing me that that pain is as much a part of the I AM THAT I AM of the Great Love, as Source is.

I tell them, *To sit with myself and love myself, brings up too much and too starkly the pain of not having been loved as a child, having to fend for myself alone in an imaginary world of faerytales* and nature. Maybe, the fact that sitting through the Tibetan's channeling is "good for me" is what bothers me the most about it!

I feel as if I know nothing, as if I am ground zero again.

Forgive me, Djwhal Khul, I say. *Forgive me, Beloveds, masters, forgive me.*

And I hear, as you readers most likely hear already, *There is nothing to forgive. Peace will come to you.*

And I beseech them, *Can you give me no answer other than "peace will come to me"?*

And they answer, *Have you not given yourself the answer, dear one? You have railed against us in your anger, confusion, impatience, and despair. All we can offer is our love, our arms to gather you in and hold you, like a flailing child.*

Do you not know that we love you? Yet, in this moment, we sense that this is not enough. You are angry with us and impatient with the time it is taking for the unfolding of this new consciousness.

Is the mighty oak impatient and angry when she beholds the pain and anguish, deaths and wars all around her? But you are not a mighty oak. You are one who sees and knows much and has much compassion. It has always been so. Always. And yet this is not the first time that you have railed against us. We have lauded the immensity of your compassion, which causes this impatience. And yet we have asked you to wait.

Can you honestly believe that those who lived in the dark ages could have heard and understood and even desired what we are heralding now?

Dear one, we love you for your compassion but please allow for the timing of the divine plan. Please allow for Source's wisdom in this. Please remember it is Source's passion play that is being enacted. Every nuance of human suffering—anguish, war, pestilence, ignorance, slow development—were and are as precious, as important in the experience of the intergalactic families, as the quarks of the ecstatic awakening into multidimensional consciousness are now.

All is interdependent, as it is necessary for evolution to occur.

Humankind had to move through its shadow experience, just as every human now must take the time to notice and take in hand, understand, and love that part that has blocked the way to this new consciousness.

In this one lifetime of yours, with all that you have been taught and all that you have learned, look at how long it has taken you to learn to truly nurture yourself. You are still learning, dear one, and there is still resistance! And this is you who have loved and worked and played amongst the masters for lifetimes!

Dear one. Precious one, beloved of us. We smile at you lovingly. Could we really have shared this new information before? You who are so evolved, yet still learning to love yourself? Could we really have shared this before?

Allow for the divine timing of Source itself, and please also remember that what you do in your own tumultuous questioning, you do for all. You are a mirror connecting us to the people. For you have much experience with us, and yet you are human, questioning and compassionate, on your path.

Can you take in, dear one (and we speak to all now), how much we love you? In this moment?

Take in this love. Surround yourself with it. Allow it, for is this not the multidimensional consciousness, now, here, always?

And, dear channel, can you take in how joyful and full of gratitude we are to you, that you have offered yourself in this way, to be in human form and bring these questions to the masters' table? And yes, dear one, you do know a good portion of the material that the Tibetan sends to all through these "chats," but perhaps you can begin to hear this material in a different way, knowing that since you were with us as master, the nuances may have changed. Allow yourself to listen through your human filter so that you can hear what those around you hear, in benefit to all.

Perhaps more importantly, notice when your ears seem closed sometimes when the suggestions of loving yourself come through.

We thank you for your courage and your earnest desire to seek the truth here, because the questions you ask here are those of many, and the answers you have received will enlighten.

It is a joy to be with you, as always.

We welcome your questions as we honor you and love you.

Go in peace now.

When I joined the workshop again and shared my anguish and morning of impatience—my process and new understanding—I was told by a seer in the group that the entire time that I was sharing, there was, as she described it, an ascended master in a white sparkling robe, impatiently pacing back and forth, back and forth, in a soft-edged globe of light, just behind me.

I was bemused by this information so I decided to write a question to the Tibetan for later that afternoon, Are the masters ever impatient?

And the Tibetan's response was, *The masters are in readiness, as if at the starting gate. They are in readiness for humans to take on this new consciousness.*[13]

The next two channelings with the Tibetan I was able to hear with crystal clarity. Something had shifted in me, and I am grateful for that shift. I eagerly await more information and conversation with the masters, and the master in myself.

I thank the masters and my own master self for this teaching.

Thank you, in the name of the light.

Thank you.

24

THEY WHO LIGHT THE EARTH

January 10, 2012

I am feeling closely the presence of the beings who live beneath the earth. I want to know more about them as I am certain they have wisdom to impart. Here, I call upon a "man" who is not human, who appeared first to me in a dream in which I climbed down a long ladder that went deep into the earth and met him.

I call forth a new light. It is unseen. It is all around us. It is in our hearts, coming from Source itself and Source inside of us.

I call forth also those of light who have been with me recently, for I have been called, more and more, to speak for the beneath-the-earth people. I have walked in the woods and felt their magic. I have heard their words. I have felt one with them, and they have asked that I share with all what they bring me.

I have searched for the correct term for these people, and I have come to "beneath-the-earth-people." It may or may not be their true name but it describes them. They can take the form of and merge into many beings on the surface of this planet: the stone people, the tree people, the leaves, the earth, the wind, water, using their eyes and ears and senses to learn much that happens here on the surface.

The one about whom I dreamt is a father, with a family, all living beneath the earth. He has given me so much love. I ask him now to speak, for he has been coming through all morning. He comes through even now, through me.

The beneath-the-earth-person speaks: *Greetings! Is that not what humans used to say long ago? Amongst my people, my formal title is Speaker. I do not use what you might call "spoken words," and yet I hold the stories, and I form a silent spoken-in-light-language link with those humans whom we have called they-who-light-the-earth.*

This one, this channel, is one of these whom we call they-who-light-the-earth. We also call her she-who-walks-the-land, for we feel her close above us, as she crunches underfoot the hoar frost crystals which spread like icy fingers on the surface of the winter woods.

It was dark this morning, in her world. There was what you call snow in the air, crystalline forms of moisture. With our etheric ears, we heard her say, Why is it so dark? When will the sun come out?

I began to impart to her the indescribable beauty of the light where we live. Although the sun's rays of light do not reach us here beneath the earth, there is an indescribable beauty of etheric light—soft, gentle, glowing, warm, pervasive—that is the light within us, that comes from the Hidden Source, the mother darkness.

How can I explain that there is light in the darkness?

I ask you readers to look within you now, deep inside the eternal caves of your own beings. There is no visible light that your physical eyes can see there. And yet, allow yourselves to look closer, as we have not forgotten how to do.

Allow yourselves to look right into the depths of the very core of your being, deep inside of you, and see your own crystalline cave of the most beautiful etheric light. Perhaps it does not feel like a cave to you. Perhaps it feels merely like a glow, or a pinpoint, at first.

This light is the light of all. It is the light of Oneness. It is the light of the loving, living Source. And this light is what links you to the light of Source for all time.

I am basking in it now, as I attempt to form the human words and terms to describe something that is indescribable! Within this light, there is a welling of joy, and peace, and delight. There is creativity here, and destiny. There are riches beyond description, for all is possible in this light.

For you humans, all you have to do is close your eyes and look for it, and you will find it. It is there in all beings.

I laugh with joy. You will hear. You will understand. Perhaps you will laugh as I describe it! This light is made up of all of the particles of loving information of the living network that connects all things, all beings, all races, all planets, all realms, the angelic realm, the intergalactic families, all universes, parallel and otherwise.

It connects all, in its breadth, its vitality, its aliveness, its gentleness, its indescribable beauty.

As each one of you recognizes this light which fills the body that is your dwelling place, each of you may see and describe it very differently, for each of you sees through a different facet of the crystalline form that created us all.

She-who-walks-the-land, the channel here today, yesterday walked in the woods near her physical home, near what she calls "Castle in the Mists." She found herself walking to a new place, sitting against a moss-covered rock that completely supported her back as she sat on the earth beside us. Yes, I say "beside us," for we were there with her.

She simply held her hands open, palms up, on the earth and began to listen, to notice, to hear and sense the vital aliveness all around her. She described it as invisible particles smaller than faery dust, each one alive, almost like a buzzing of bees, everywhere around her.

This is the vital aliveness of the trees, the wind, the leaves, the stone people, the root people, the animals, the devas and faeries and elementals, even the far blue mountain—she could feel its aliveness, although it was miles away.

This ability that she is growing, remembering, is what we have known for all time, for we were the first people of this Planet Earth.

We were born of the mud. We were born of the stone. We have form and yet we are formless enough to merge with all things. And so we witness all that passes here on the planet's surface.

Is this not what they-who-light-the-earth are bringing to this planet now, remembering for this planet, for the collective consciousness now: remembering and reconnecting with their abilities to see and hear and sense and experience this living network of light that is Source itself?

We are the keepers of the crystals. Our light-thoughts move through the crystals, amplify and spread throughout the entire living network, through the tendrils of the roots beneath the earth, right into the living sap, the life blood of the great ones. Imparting across the planet the words that are not words, the thoughts that are not thoughts, the joy beyond joy itself, the light beyond light as, with your etheric eyes, dear ones, you are learning to see it now within you.

We love. We have families. We play.

We listen. We anchor the information that comes to us through the light-channel of this living network, and we bring it through our light-thoughts—with intention—to the crystals, to the crystalline field where it is recorded for all time. It is somewhat like your akashic records, the records of your individual souls. And yet, these are the light-records of this planet. In these light-records is known all that has come, all that is coming. The particles of detail are added as they also come, as they are also known.

And you, dear ones who walk the earth now, as you allow yourselves to tap into the light within you, as you learn to listen and sense as we do, you add to your understanding and experience of multidimensional reality, as part of the living network that you are.

This beautiful Planet Earth, this beautiful planet is transforming so quickly through you humans. All of this can occur faster than the speed of light, yet we must slow the light information enough so that we can form it into words, into thoughts and ideas, so that you who are beginning to see and hear and understand can join us and all of those who bring light to the earth, in understanding and spreading the news.

The channel has asked me to tell you of my family. I have so much love for them. I have a beautiful mate, and a boy child and a girl child. And it is our joy to sit at the table, for there are times when we call she-who-walks-the-land in to join us at our table, as we do now. And she sees and feels the laughter and the light-filled teasing. There is no jab in the teasing here. It is very playful.

I, as storyteller, tell my dear mate and my children of my silent conversations with this channel. I tell them of everything that she-who-walks-the-land above tells me and experiences and learns.

I tell them of her struggle that speaks for humanity's struggle, to learn to trust the divine timing that runs through this living network like sap, like blood in the veins of all beings, blood in the veins of this planet.

This living vitality moves towards a unilateral multidimensionality that transcends all war, pestilence, disease, hatred, all of those pieces of shadow that this planet through humankind has offered to experience, move through, and purge for Source itself. For have not many said that all of this activity of the shadow emerging and purging and clearing—although it appears unnecessary—does add to the wealth of experience of Source, and to our own love and compassion and that indescribable beauty of the light within?

And when we speak of the light within, are we not describing blind faith? Is not blind faith seeing with other than physical eyes? If you were to look inside at this moment, with your multidimensional eyes, would you not see the light within you? And is this not seeing faith itself, faith seeing itself in the light within you?

Allow this now.

Faith in your own inner light is the belief in your ability to love the unknown and find it within yourself, in your knowing. For is Source itself not a great knowing that continues to learn through you, through us, through all members of the intergalactic families, the angelic realm, the masters, and all beings in all universes?

Yes, we hear you, the channel, ask about the aborigines in Australia, that place that has been named Australia by those who speak English. Yes, they are of our family and, yes, you readers are of our family. And, yes, the faeries and devas and elementals, the tree people and root people and stone people, the four-leggeds, those who swim, those who crawl upon the earth—yes, all are of our family.

There is an indescribable joy within me as I say to you, dear ones, readers, channel, that this family that I describe, that I have said, yes, they belong—dear ones, this is the family of Source itself! A family joined in joy, joined in love beyond limit, joined in indi-

vidual and united experience, joined in laughter, and memory, and the records that we share!

This channel, she-who-walks-the-land, was born as an identical twin. She tracks the time that she and her twin have shared, from the moment when their single egg was formed in the womb of their physical mother. Dear ones, the existence of all beings in the living network is tracked in the crystalline records. And, just as the twins track their existence to the time shared in the egg, the crystalline records track our existence, each one of us, each one of you, all the way back to the time we shared as Source itself.

Feel this. Know this now in this moment. Allow yourselves now to take in the truth that the crystalline records track your history all the way back—past-present-future-parallel-lifetimes—all the way back, dear ones, to being more than just part of Source, but rather Source itself.

It is time now, dear ones, to retrieve, remember, and reconnect with the experience of that time then, as Source, just as it is time to begin to connect through your every sense with your place in the living network, so that you can at last experience being, in the same breath, both Source and individual self.

It is impossible to describe in human words—in light-language, light-thought, any form, any picture or sound—the immensity of the joy that Source feels, emanates, and transmits, in its knowledge of your experience of union with it.

Allow this joy to permeate your existence.

This joy is home. This joy is where you belong.

You are a part of the living network, dear ones, with every breath, every moment of your existence. Every piece of information that travels through you on the living network expands the joy of Source itself, in Source's recognition of all that you are and all that you add to its being, and thus to the family of Source!

Allow the truth of this to fill the light within you.

Allow the truth of this to transmit across this living network to all who may unconsciously or consciously seek it, and to all who are as yet unawakened.

Allow it to breathe into their dreams. Allow it to breathe into their vision. Perhaps in a sunset. Perhaps in the running of a deer in the woods. Perhaps in a smile that reminds them of something that they cannot place, that they have forgotten but that is linked to the living light inside of them and draws them to the awakening that is happening now.

Dear ones, listen. Notice. Hear. See.

Allow your expansion, your link, your part in this living network that is the multidimensional consciousness of Source itself.

Name yourself as a member of the family of Source. For are we not brothers and sisters of this unity, of this Oneness?

Let us rejoice in this knowing!

Let us rejoice in this knowing!

I ask also that those of you who cannot find a heart connection with, or who feel some friction or abrasion between you and another human or between you and news on your television set or radio—between you and any other substance—I ask that you notice that.

Rather than going directly to judgment, or fear, or anger, or even if you do go to those places first, I ask that you remind yourself that we are all part of the same living network, and then love yourself.

Send love to whatever the feeling is, even if it does not feel compatible at this time. Notice what happens within your being. There is an image now of a pool of water that absorbs a clod of mud that is that discomfort and, slowly, it becomes one with the water. In the same way are we all one with Source.

We ask that you attempt to do this. If you would like to look more into the reasons for your discomfort, do so. That is up to you.

My children, my mate, the others of us who are the beneath-the-earth people, we thank the channel today. We thank you, our readers.

We smile with love and gratitude at the chance to share with you a little of who we are and to let you know that we are here with you as you take every step on the planet. Even those of you who live in an environment of concrete pavement, we feel you. We record your experience in the crystalline structures, here beneath the earth.

I, Speaker, thank all of the beneath-the-earth people for sharing their light-thoughts, their own living network ideas, with me to transmit to you through human words. It is our wish that you take this transmission with love, knowing that we are your brothers and sisters in love. We ask that you go in peace, and the joy in the knowledge of your place in the family of Source and all beings.

Thank you in the name of the light within you and within all.

Go in peace now, dear ones. Go in peace.

I am so full of joy and delight at the idea of being a member of the family of Source! What a huge family I suddenly have!

Also, it helps me to understand that if I can see all beings as part of the living network, I can begin to let go of the inner discord I feel in the presence of some people. This is something I continue to work on, through journaling, praying, and talking with others, both master and human. I want to be in a place of peace within myself, along with or even in spite of those around me.

After this channeling, I asked the Speaker of the beneath-the-earth people for his name. He told me his name was Glyph. *Webster's Ninth New Collegiate Dictionary* defines Glyph as follows: "a symbol… that conveys information nonverbally."[14] A perfect name for the Speaker for those who keep the records!

I cannot thank Glyph enough for sharing his beautiful words with me and with all of us.

25

ON THE PATH

OF THE BELOVED

January 13, 2012

I was supposed to be shoveling snow this morning and doing my accounts, but I was moved to do this channeling, which comes from my own master self.

And so, I call in the assistance of those of light—the masters, the angelic realm, Vywamus, Yeshu, Magdalen, Germaine, Quan Yin,[G] the Tibetan—and I also call forth that most beautiful, highest evolutionary light that is the light of Source itself, within and without, and all around us. And I ask to be surrounded by a sphere of that light, that this room become a sphere of that light.

I call forth now my highest speaker self who can, with clarity, share my thoughts of this morning.

At the end of the last session, the Speaker for the beneath-the-earth people suggested that when there is someone with whom we don't feel comfortable, we might hand the difficulty or discomfort around that one, to the light, to Source. He said this for me and for all of us who have an abrasion or friction with some other person, or object, thought, or energy.

It really struck me this morning how I have had such a difficult time with one person in my life. What I want to say here is that if I remind myself that our individual records track back to a time when we were all Source, as One in the beginning, something changes within me about that person.

I begin to see her as one of the many who are the family of Source itself. I begin to feel the energy of the splintering of Source, into the sparks that each one of us became, and I follow that path energetically, without pictures or words or specific content. I follow the path of all of these sparks of light that are Source, and I see the one with whom I have friction. I see that she has merely been following her path, as I have been following mine.

True, they are not the same path. And, yes, there is friction, but do I need to understand her path? Can I not just accept that we are not alike, that our paths are not the same? I do not have to be on her path and she does not have to be on mine.

Can there not still be a oneness of love, a detached impersonal love between us, rather than the attachment of a cord of friction and the self-questioning that asks what is wrong with me that I cannot comfortably be in her presence?

Something shifts in me when I understand this, when I realize that I have no responsibility to share her path, or to be friends, or choose her company, or welcome her to my bosom. I have no responsibility to do any of that.

I do have the responsibility, however, as a member of the family of Source, to have love for all members. It does not have to be a personal love. It does not have to be a love of action, or words, or gifts, or praise, or camaraderie, or friendship. It can be merely a generic love, in the understanding that we all come from the individual experience of Source itself.

This responsibility of love for every member of the family of Source—whether or not the members are named or known or seen or heard, or interacted with—holds no guilt or debt. It holds only the freedom of Source, that is part of that love, the freedom that allows us to take the path that we choose—or that is chosen by our soul self, in our desire to learn.

I am beginning to understand and feel the meaning of my book title, *On the Path of the Beloved*.

If we are each a member of the family of Source and thus can track our lineage, our records, back to a time before Source created us, then the pathway that each of us takes from the moment that we began is a path of the beloved, that the Beloved Source itself in each of us travels to completion, wherever that path may lead.

That completion is our multidimensional ability to be Source itself, at the same time as we are individuals.

So, "the beloved," dear ones, is each of us. Whatever path we take, it cannot but be the path of the beloved. Even friction, or the abrasion of a relationship, is a part of that path, and adds to the living network of Source itself and all beings. Can I not allow that it is so, and yet see both self and other as beloved, even if I have no interactions with that other?

I ask the masters now if there is anything else they might want to add. I feel, see, sense, the circle smiling. I hear, see, sense the word "COMPLETION."

They want, and I want, for this transmission to be complete at this time, as short as it is, because it is so important to the masters and my master self. It is especially important for this channel, for the "I" of the I AM THAT I AM, who speaks here.

Speaking for the masters now, I say, *Thank you.*
And welcome to the family of Source.

26

THE DIVINE FEMININE

January 13, 2012

It seems as if I am coming full circle, since the last chapter was the title of this book, and now I am re-thinking some aspects of the divine feminine too.

I am beginning to wonder about why we humans separate the divinity or Source into "divine feminine" and "divine masculine." Are there lines drawn between them in Source's view shed? Are they not One, as we all are? Is not love itself, and all experience, that of the One and individual in each of us?

Magdalen responds here: *While I do speak for the divine feminine, I also speak for the Oneness of Source and so I will attempt to define that which truly has no concrete definition, dear one. Humans and other beings have divided the divinity into two genders, because the human experience, as well as the experience of some others of the intergalactics, is also divided in that way.*

Our purpose is not to endorse further misunderstanding but to do all in our power to assist humanity, and other beings, in understanding, owning, and integrating the concept of being an individual Source Self, at the same time as being Source, the Oneness itself.

There is an infinite number of qualities belonging to Source. For some, to even begin to fathom what Source is goes beyond their abilities of imagination or conscious experience.

Yeshu came as a human man, and his mother Mary and I came as human women because there are those who relate more to a mother or father figure for identity, for intimacy, rather than a formless universal being, such as Source.

Much is said here in these writings about the divine feminine. Some aspects we have not mentioned include harboring, being patient, allowing, nurturing, gestating, surrendering, and being rather than doing. Aspects of the divine masculine include clarity, discernment, doing, thinking, creating, formulating, designing, planning, analyzing, directing, manifesting, and so on.

Please realize, dear readers, that we are not speaking of the masculine qualities in human men, or the feminine qualities in human women. We are speaking of the qualities of the divine masculine and divine feminine themselves, many of which are inherent in all men and women. A human man will have aspects of the feminine, as well as the masculine, just as a human woman will have aspects of the masculine, as well as the feminine.

Some have attributed negative aspects to the masculine. For instance, being tough, violent, mean, demeaning to women, lewd, and so on. Some have attributed negative aspects to the feminine, such as being clingy, submissive, whining, weak, or vain. None of these qualities pertain to the divine masculine or divine feminine. These negative aspects apply to the basest of feminine and masculine qualities in humanity.

There is a great difference between the base feminine—ascribed to females—and the divine feminine which is an aspect of the divine, just as between the base masculine—ascribed to males—and the divine masculine which is also an aspect of the divine.

The combination of the divine feminine and the divine masculine may be called the divine union and, when they are in balance in a person, there is then a wholeness of being.

We are speaking of the most highly evolved qualities of the masculine and feminine, as emanating from the divine itself. There is no judgment here, only an effort to bring all into clarity in the fold of the family of Source.

To intuit more, one may use what is called the higher mind which is directly connected to one's divine consciousness or soul and offers illumination and a greater understanding. The higher mind can be accessed through meditation or intention and is more traditionally associated with the divine masculine, just as any mental faculty is.

Others may open their high heart which is directly connected to the heart of Source and offers profound love and acceptance while expanding one's sensate awareness of the divine. The high *heart is accessed through prayer or attention to joy and is more often associated with the divine feminine.*

Again, having well-developed aspects of both divine feminine and divine masculine is intrinsically necessary for a well-balanced whole in any given person.

January 13, 2012

The masters speak: *We would never attempt to disallow any efforts on humanity's part to describe and give form to the great formlessness, which is Source. Many humans have a need to make order out of chaos, to delineate and to list the qualities of Source, to set one quality in one column of the balance sheet and another in the other, to create an equal number in each column. This is done in an attempt to feel the comfort and pleasing effect of an ordered balance of known quantities, separated out of the great unknown.*

We smile lovingly and with complete acceptance, and even devotion, at your very human quest to know! We delight in it! At the same time, there is truly no three-dimensional way to describe or order or define Source, the Unknowable, the Great Love, as many have called it.

Indeed, here in the halls of the masters, the terms "divine feminine" and "divine masculine" are not used, but rather the "divine magnetism," which draws all beings along their paths towards the experience of being, in the same moment, both Source and individual Source Self, on all multidimensional planes, levels, and dimensions.

In fact, the experience of being both the Oneness and one of Source's individual Source Selves in the multidimensional consciousness you are moving into, makes humanity's terms "divine feminine" and "divine masculine" obsolete! For it is the combined qualities of the two that offer the balance of wholeness. And it is to this wholeness that all existence is moving, for is not all existence Source itself?

Humanity is still attempting to find nameable pigeonholes in the unknowable experience of Source.

Do not give up your query, dear ones. For all information, all answers, lie along the path and add to its grace and glory. We are only answering the question put to us by the channel. And this is merely what we offer to you through the filter of the channel. You must decide the truth for yourselves, dear ones. It is yours and yours alone, as are all your truths!

February 28, 2012

The fact is that we are human. Whether three-dimensional or multidimensional, I live in a human body, and I have the experience of mother and father, male and female.

There is a desire in me to refute this humanness for the experience of being Source, solely, for whom the essence of mother and father are one. I can refute all I want but the reality of my humanity and my gender remain. I ask that this thought-field remain open that more wisdom will come.

27

THE "SIN" OF OBESITY

January 22, 2012

What a shaming label the word "obese" is. Here I am living in a time of multidimensional transformation, a place of grace and beauty and enhanced awareness, as part of a living network in the family of Source. And yet, the energy of labels and judgment hovers in the ethers around this planet, and I want somehow to see a transformation take place there too.

I have had a "weight issue" most of my life. I am tired of being magic on the inside and weighted down, heavy, in my physical body. At last, I am familiar enough with loving myself, knowing myself, that I feel I can look at this issue, as a next step on the path of treating myself as a beloved.

Can loving myself actually heal my physical body? I seek assistance, guidance, and insight from the masters on this.

I call in the highest, most beautiful crystalline light within, of Source itself, the highest evolutionary light to this point now, which we know is rapidly changing and transforming.

I call in the highest part of my self, my Source Self, speaker for the collective consciousness, if you will. I am smiling, for do we not each speak for our own facet of the collective consciousness, in our questioning, in our thirst on this voyage, this path of the beloved?

I am sitting in what I call the "keep" of my castle. The fire is newly laid. There is snow on the mountains. The sun sparkles on the snow with many colors. Do we judge the size of the snow crystals, or the trees, or the log in the fire, except to discern how well the fire will burn?

I am struck by the western medical term "obesity." It is a horror, a shame, a sin, a violation, physical proof of a lack of will! It is an abomination! I hope that you realize these are not my words. These are words, though, that I have heard spoken —by doctors, my mother, and acquaintances.

When a child is born, and the baby is chubby, people smile and say, Look at those chubby little legs. Look at those chubby little hands and chubby little cheeks! Aren't they cute? Isn't she sweet?

Why is that not said of us as we get older?

Healthy infants are hungry for being touched, held, and fed in a loving way. Some infants learn to link food—the mother's breast and the milk produced—with love. Some infants have experienced no love, and grasp as at straws for the only love or the only comfort they can find. It may come as food or warmth or, perhaps soothing sounds, soothing images.

I have recently reread the chapter about the loving mother within, and the "Transmission of Love." I am especially intrigued by the immensity of the broad hips, the broad welcome breasts and arms of the being that calls herself the loving mother within, who resembles the Goddess of Willendorf.

I know that she is with me here, in this telling.

I have been exploring my own weight, considering eating less, having smaller portions, exercising more—all of those things that many have advised me and others to do, in order to lose weight. Even though I want to evolve in this area, I feel especially vulnerable writing about it and yet it feels right to do so at this time. For all.

There is something here about the word "comfort" and about the loving mother within, and loving yourself. As I feel her come in, I sink now again into that loving mother within being, who is both an archetype and developing within me. I will step aside now, so that she can speak.

Loving mother within, speaking for the Mother and all loving mothers within: *Dear child of the Beloveds. Dear beloveds who read our words.*

She who has channeled us before and channels us today has been mulling over many thoughts that have come through from us, from her own master self, from Source, from different places on the planet and beneath the earth, and from many lifetimes.

There are so many fallacies involved in the "issue of obesity," especially in this country, the United States. Dear ones, we wish for you to know—and my heart opens and expands greatly, in compassion for you all—that it is so very important that you learn to give yourself comfort. To give yourself nurturing, to honor and cherish yourself and listen to yourself.

There is no set regimen by which to eat what you call "food," what we call "nourishment." The only thing that we ask of you is that, when preparing something for yourself to eat, you ask yourself and listen to what it is you truly want in the moment. It is not the physical action of eating that gives the nourishment. It is the conscious comforting and caring for the child within and the entire being that you are, while eating, that creates the nourishment.

It is not about a habit of eating certain foods over and over again, because they are known and easy to prepare, and you have forgotten whether or not you even like them. It is about truly listening to yourself: What do I want right now? Does this that I am used to really taste good? Does this really nourish me? Do I really want this?

For in the same way that there is an expansion of sensitivity and the senses around this new multidimensionality, there is also embedded there the developing awareness of the whole body, the whole being.

Think of what you put into your body as a part of that living network all around you. Think about it being ego-syntonic,[G] in alignment with your whole being, not just with a correct procedure in diet, according to dieticians, vegetarians, carnivores, vegans, breatharians, or any other eating regimens.

This is not about a regimen, dear ones. This is about allowing the alignment of all things, all beings, all facets of Source itself, into perfect balance. Self-comforting is a joyful means to being one with the Oneness itself, is it not, dear ones?

There are tears in the channel's eyes that are my tears, dear ones. For I so truly want you to know this.

The other day, the channel asked a dear friend if she would prepare food for her because the channel did not want to be bothered with cooking or preparing food. Her birth mother had not wanted to prepare food, let alone prepare it lovingly, and the channel had taken on this attitude unconsciously.

The channel's dear friend said, Well, that would be difficult because I cook what I feel like having in the moment. I ask myself what would feel good to me to put into my body at this time. At that time, the channel did not understand.

But she is beginning to understand now.

If every particle of sustenance that goes into the body is something that is truly desired, is something that is known to give an expectation of true comfort, then whatever it is, whether it be fat or lean, sweet or sour, hot or cold, it is the right thing. For if you are truly listening in your whole being in a multidimensional way to learn what your being needs in the way of comfort, nurturing, and replenishment, you will know what is right for you.

I smile in my love for the Oneness all around me, for Source's beautiful great love and wisdom, for you readers and the channel, Source's individual Source Selves, as you search for understanding and wisdom in this moment, as you listen and open your hearts and your etheric ears, and your high heart minds, to understand.

When you truly receive into your being something that you know is comforting and loving, that knowledge sets off a spark, a belief, that multiplies it to the nth power and sets off a chain reaction of truth, activation, transformation, and alchemy, within you.

If you know, absolutely, in all of your being that it is a slice of toast with butter on it that will indeed give you true comfort as you bring it into your body, and as you affirm that it is comforting and loving for you to give this to yourself, then as you intend it, it becomes so.

Say, instead, dear ones—and perhaps this may sound familiar to many and many, or at least some—that you make a piece of toast with butter and rapidly cram it into your mouth and say, Oh this is so fattening, but I'm going to have it anyway.

Do you not know that that's what your body hears? That's what your being hears, that you are punishing your whole being? You are telling your body that it is to become "fat" or "fatter." Then comes the guilt and the shame, rather than the pleasing effect of nourishment, and self-care, and self-comforting.

The physical realm is such a tiny portion of the full spectrum of multidimensionality. The number of calories in a pat of butter is a part of that physical realm. Embedding self-love into that pat of butter through alchemy and intention places one directly into the living network of the multidimensional realm.

Do you understand this, dear ones? Allow yourselves to take this in. We are talking about the well known laws of attraction,^G but more than this.

We are talking about you the channel, you the readers, all Source Selves—each and every one of you—tending and attending to the needs of the being, the child, the adult, the tree, the flower, the animal. It is so easy to tend to plants, is it not? To the garden, the house. And yet, how easy is it to tend to the body, to the being, to the self?

We expect perfection because you are perfect as you are, dear ones, and at the same time, we do not expect you to do things perfectly because this is a school of multidimensionality, a school of higher learning where you are in the process of developing skills.

Many of the intergalactic families do not have bodies in three-dimensional form. The planet has offered humanity to incarnate into three-dimensional bodies. Part of the reason for this incarnation into three-dimensionality is to enhance, implement, and bring into physicality the skills of self-caring and nurturing and comforting—a thousandfold!

Yet it has been so simple for humans to turn to self-punishment and shame and guilt, rather than self-care.

We could not possibly love you more. We could not possibly wish to comfort you more. And yet, if it is only we who love and comfort you—speaking for the masters, as the loving mother within, who is both master and within you, developing—then you are left empty of the wealth that exists in the experience of loving and comforting yourselves.

For each time—and, oh, dear ones, the channel's heart chokes with the joy of this knowledge as it comes through her—each time, dear ones, that you comfort yourself, you are in fact, in that moment, being Source comforting the individual Source Self that you are.

Take this in, dear ones.

Take this in.

And know this also, dear ones: Each time you transmit love to another being, that energy of love radiates out and adds another sound-wave to the frequency of love that surrounds this planet. Imagine now that you add to that frequency, not through the energy of your self-punishment or guilt or shame but through your loving yourself instead! Imagine how you strengthen and amplify that frequency for all beings, all universes!

Take in the magnitude of this statement.

Allow yourself to be Source now in this moment, desiring above all things to offer comfort, love, and gentle nurturing to your individual Source Self. This is who you are in this lifetime which is a simple linear moment in your entire divine existence.

Now, see the effect in your mind's eye of the gift of your love to the planet and all beings in all universes.

This is so important, dear ones. We are so glad that the channel has been tumbling these thoughts in her mind, questioning, turning this over, wondering, how she can do this for herself.

So many times, the channel, when eating unconsciously, has dumped food into herself, treating her body—the temple of her soul—as a trash can. A plate of food is not just "matter" that goes into the trash can of your belly. No, dear ones.

Do you know the depth of Source's grief and compassion, when it beholds a beloved's shame when that one is labeled "obese?"

Dear ones, allow yourselves to don the velvet robe embedded with crystals that belongs to your Source Self, as you sit before a table, having prepared for yourself a meal comprised of nourishment that comforts your very soul.

Allow yourself to see the plate of food with your soul's eyes, or even your imagination! See it transform into comfort, nourishment, and self-love. As you partake of the plate, allow it to alchemize into the multidimensional truth of Source itself loving you.

The more that you allow yourself to experience this feeling in your entire being, the more it becomes an initiation of love, transforming you. You move further along your path of the beloved, to your own Source experience of loving yourself, as one in the multidimensional realm of all beings, and also as the dear inner child who receives the love of both the master within and the loving mother within.

For in the moment when the plate on the table becomes an initiation of love, you yourself, along with the loving mother within, have consciously mastered the ability to nurture the whole being.

Dear ones, I ask that you truly take in this image of you as loving mother within offering to yourself an initiation of love.

I would now also extend this to those who have not been called "obese," or who do not consider themselves overweight, or have no issue with their weight. Truly, weight has nothing to do with this transmission. But it became a platform from which we could explain this entire element of transformation into loving and comforting the self.

Dear ones, we are not just talking about a plate of food. The same is true for taking a hot bath and allowing yourself to feel that bath, allowing yourself to linger in that tub.

Or sitting on a stone in the woods, looking out to the far mountains and allowing that moment, and naming it as comfort, as nourishment for the physical self, the soul, the individual Source Self, and the entire being.

Or watching a movie, or reading a book, for fun or comfort, or because that is what the child wants to do at the time.

We are talking about attending and comforting. For is not comforting something that the loving mother within does?

We are so grateful to the channel for having brought this issue and these thoughts forward. We are so grateful to you readers for being here to complete this activation and to bring it full circle.

Without you, our words would not come.

We have spoken this before.

We ask you merely to delight in all facets of yourself.

There is no judgment here. There is no way to do it wrong.

There is no such thing as a straight A^+ in this school! We are laughing! For if there is, you all get A^+'s, all along the way, dear ones, for we joyously love every moment of your exploration.

With so much love, light, and gratitude, we leave you now.
Go in peace, dear ones.
Go in peace.
Blessings to you.

I can't help but say, *Thank you, Beloveds, for your wisdom here. It helps so much to have this much more insight into self-nurturing.*

There are two things that I would like to add here. The first, very briefly but very importantly, is the terror experienced by a child, or an inner child, when confronted with the withholding of comfort through the withholding of food, whether to lose weight, or as punishment, or something else.

In the case of the rigid, regimental diets still often prescribed by the western world, there can arise a feeling of absolute terror when one is told that he or she is not allowed to have those foods, those treats—that unconscious comfort—that one is used to having. It is the child part of us that is comforted, or feels the denial of comfort and then reacts.

When some people think about going on a diet, they can experience absolute terror. I have. For me, the terror is my inner child's frozen belief that the only comforting or nurturing substance that she knew growing up will be taken away, and there will be nothing to replace it. She will be helpless, comfortless, and powerless to do anything about it.

At the other end of the spectrum is the other piece I want to add here: the incredible feeling of total interdependence and harmony when treating that plate of food as a part of the multidimensional experience.

It is a profound experience to be consciously aware of and grateful to the cow that offered its milk to create the butter, the human process of making the bread and the butter (I am assuming organic for all of this), and the earth that fed the cow and wheat, rye, quinoa—whatever it is—that created the grain, that became the bread that is buttered.

The act of noticing all of this and having gratitude for those beings who are a part of—and who offered themselves to create—this plate of food puts us directly in the stream of the living network.

In being consciously aware of this process, we are ingesting multiple pieces of the living network at the same time as we are part of it. We become a part of the whole in that way, a link in the chain of the living network, part of the loving contract between all beings, and Source itself. There is a transformation that takes place here, when we sit at a meal, aware of this piece.

January 23, 2012

When I am thinking of food, I can now ask myself, what is it that I want? Am I looking to feed myself because I am hungry? Or is it that I am looking for comfort in food?

If it is comfort I am looking for, I wonder if I can then look to the comfort of the loving mother within, or of Source itself?

Or is it that food is the only thing that can comfort me in this moment? And what is it that makes me yearn for comfort right now? Do I need to know, or can I simply be aware of the fact that it is some kind of comforting that I seek?

My Source Self, as loving mother within, speaks to all here: *Fill yourself with the joy of the everlasting love that is all around you. Know that you are loved and fill yourself with this knowing. Curl up in the mother darkness and allow yourself to be held in the divinity and grace of Source itself.*

Take the one moment needed to affirm your place in the family of Source and revel in the fact that you are not alone.

If it is boredom that drives you to the need for comfort, allow one of us (masters) to step to your side and share in whatever you are doing right now. Or allow your master self to remember your loving mother within and let her/us experience the boredom with you! Does the boredom change? Does it stay? What happens? Experiment with this, for is this time now not one of great experiments?

If it is fear, again, let her/us stand beside you, and hold you in the fear, and share it with you until it subsides and you can feel our love. Perhaps then you can know what it is that you fear.

And if it is truly that the inner child of you seeks comfort through a piece of chocolate or a piece of bread, allow yourself to recognize that as you feed the child, you are loving and comforting that child. Allow yourself the conscious awareness of your role in this, dear ones.

There is no one more dear to us, each and every one of you, in every moment of your experience.

Know this.
Take in the truth of this.
Allow this.
You tend the fire. Why wouldn't you tend yourselves, dear ones?

28

BODY BELOVED

February 11, 2012

    How still it is, here on the mountain.
    My ears and whole being hear and feel the living network.
    I feel like a blank slate, waiting for a truth to come.
    I realize again that walking in nature is not so much about exercise as it is about connecting with myself. Even this short walk to the view at the top of my little mountain gives me the gift of myself, in the stillness here.
    I can barely hear the traffic below, so muted and Saturday-absent that it could be the sound of a distant stream. A tiny spider traverses my leg and reminds me that we are sisters, members of the same lineage of Source. I mentally search my house for a place as perfect as nature to write in and the search, despite all of my renovations, ends in a blank. And yet the writing comes.

I am held in the crook of a makeshift child's fort of plywood, and my view is the far-off blue mountain, so camouflaged in vertical stripes of hemlock that I can barely see it. It is the gently loving, silent, snow-dusted hemlocks themselves that hold me in this stillness. I need nothing else at this moment.

I can feel the hemlocks, I "hear" a buzz of activity/awareness in my etheric ears, and I wonder that this is so sweetly familiar; and yet my own body is a stranger to me, almost as if it is a separate entity and does not belong to me. I want to change that relationship if I can. I want to love my body, as Magdalen loved hers.

When I wrote *Love Incarnate*, I began, "Yeshu, I would know you."[15] It makes me weep, now.

I suppose I will try those same words again.

Body, I would know you. An endless, bottomless void opens out before me. I get an immediate headache.

The Body speaks: *When I, the body, was small, the consciousness of my person shut down to me, closed itself off from me. At that time, there were the sensations of physical and genital pain, hunger in the belly, a chafed, wet, cold bottom. The child's consciousness could not hold or contain this information.*

Sensation existed as if in a vacuum and was transmitted by the brain, but not received by the child self. Her soul's force field would not allow it. If the sensations had been received, the child self would have died or lost her mind.

This process made me a dead thing.

It piled the layers upon layers of unconscious luminous thought substance of the child on top of me, between the child self's consciousness and me, so that no matter how loudly I screamed, she could not hear or feel me.

Over the years, as more painful things happened to her, she turned her back on me completely.

Now, she wants to know me. How can I trust this? There is a coldness of affect here, in me. In her.

She can love the being that she is, but not the physical house she lives in.

She wonders how to love me.

Perhaps if she learned what I do for her. I hold in this belly, here, not only the fat, but also the physicality of her memories, cellular records of which she has little or no conscious knowledge. The memories are embedded energetically in her second chakra, which the belly of this physical body surrounds.

Perhaps when the judgments come, about the belly or some other part of me, she might allow them, instead of resisting them, and then she might listen to and move through them, to me.

Perhaps if she sat or stood in front of a mirror and cupped her face, as she did twenty years ago, and looked into her own eyes— the eyes of this body that I am—she could learn to see and love the beauty that I am, that I see.

Perhaps if she spoke to her belly and put her arms around it, and thanked it for protecting her by holding itself separate from the child, separate from all the memories.

Perhaps if she noticed and thanked every finger, every toe, ankle, knee, thigh, every part of this that I am—her body that harbors her soul and being and allows her to move forward and evolve with grace, into her true Self.

Perhaps then she could love me.

There is a whisper of just a trace of recognition of this last statement that repeats what the child used to say about her parents: Perhaps if I did this, or said that, then they would love me.

The chasm between her and me is almost limitless. I say "almost" because there is now a tiny spark of hope. All that I have been through—left alone with the sensations of it—has created this separation. There has been an unspeakable terror in the child, now woman, in even contemplating the joining with me, for fear of having to face those same sensations after all this time.

I tell her, Here I am, willing and ready to help in any way I can. Already the senses have come forward to inform her of our connection. Does she not know that the senses come from me?

I ask that all those of light who are here at this time, especially her angelic team, help her to treat me kindly. This is really almost all that I ask. I say "almost" because I do not know, myself, what I might want. I am not accustomed to being heard in this.

I do ask that she be aware, merely, when she shovels food into the mouth without thinking. It feels terribly unkind and invasive to me. It comes as a shock. There is no communication of need, or want, or desire. It is as if she is saying, I will stuff this into the body to shut up the feelings.

Does she not know that the body is not the feelings?

Does she not know that she feels through *the body?* It is the body that gives her the physical messages that come with the feelings, the tightness in the throat when afraid, the twisting in the belly with dread, the heart pressing against the rib cage in joy.

When she shovels the food into me, she is attempting to escape from the feelings that she senses—with a sixth sense that is not of my province—will be too painful. It is the child self who has suddenly emerged, who senses the imminent presence of the lurking, looming buried sensations of long ago, which she thinks will engulf her so that she will disappear or even die.

The reality is that all it does, when she stuffs something into the mouth like that, bolting and gulping it, is dump something foreign (because the senses have not been prepared) into the belly, thereby strangling me for a moment as she forces the esophagus to swallow it into the belly. That which lurks is put in abeyance, and the child and her feelings disappear, and are buried again—unseen, unheard, unhealed—and then the woman feels the remorse of the dumping.

But the feelings are not stored in the belly. The food is. The feelings go into the second chakra and the ethers in the cells around that chakra that are held within the physicality of the belly. When the feelings are choked back, replaced by the sensation of dumping food into the belly, the energy flow to that chakra is blocked, stuffed.

When blocked, neither second chakra gateway, front or back, can breathe light or song into the feeling, as would have happened if the *adult had allowed it, so that it could be felt, moved through, learned from, and transmuted into light.*

The immensity of the process terrifies and daunts this woman, the process of scrutinizing and digesting in this way all of the feelings of the memories that are stored in the second chakra. The blocks she has created by resisting the feelings have leaked their energy into different parts of the body closest to the second chakra, her uterus—now gone—her pelvis, lower back, hips, and knees, all arthritic.

Does she not know that every piece of memory does not have to be scrutinized? She can ask me for assistance in gently opening the floodgates to the body's sensations of these feelings so she can let them go. It is the senses that link the body to the self. This is new information for her.

What is the sensation of sadness? She knows it well: tightening of the throat, a feeling of tears welling in the chest, overflowing down into the solar plexus and up into the throat, and a sick feeling in the belly. These are the sensations I experience. Perhaps, other bodies have other sensations of sadness but I can only name my own.

I have always been here, trying to help her with all of this. Perhaps she can feel me here, now. In the writing of this is her intent and her belief in the possibility that perhaps I am not a stranger to her after all. Perhaps I am an ally, a friend, a link to the living network of this lifetime, through sensation.

I thank her, and all, for this opportunity to speak. And I thank her for her willingness to listen and to hear what I have said today. She has found her way to me, at last. I am glad.

February 12, 2012

It continues to astound me how much I don't know.

About an hour ago, I went outside to bring wood in for the fire, and the sensation of a cold head suggested to me that I go and get a hat.

I had no idea that this body, who has been a stranger to me, actually needs me to take care of it. It cannot take care of itself without the self being conscious of the body's needs! This is such a revolutionary idea to me. Most likely it is second nature to most others.

It has just now dawned on me that the body cannot use the legs to get the hat, the arms to put it on, without the self being conscious and hearing the message sent by the body via the senses, telling the self what the body needs to be maintained in a healthy way.

And eating: absolutely amazing the hub-bub of details involved in having a meal!

First is the prayer of gratitude to all of the components of the living network, which have offered themselves to assimilate with the whole being—the individual Source Self and the physical body that houses it.

Just now, the menu is salad, with shredded carrots and beets, sprouts, mixed baby greens, and goat cheese, all organic. If there is consciousness, there are a myriad of sensations! Mirabile dictu!!![16]

There is the hand raising the bite of food to the mouth.

Then, there is the chewing: the grinding between the molars, the trickling down of the heavenly juices into the esophagus, the awareness of the food being ground finer and finer, so that there is a gentleness about the stomach's receipt and subsequent digestion of it.

The sudden bursting of flavor transmits from the taste buds of the body, with a message of pleasure to the brain, an affirmative message that says this is what the body wants. Physical body? Most likely, since it is salad, but the emotional body too is experiencing a soothing sensation from the softness and fullness of the creamy, buttery goat cheese.

The self wonders about the stomach, decides to see if it can feel any sensation at all that identifies that the stomach is anything other than dead, as it has always been, except when the self stuffs it beyond fullness. Then, the body's stomach yells so loud in pain that the self can actually feel the sensation of overfilled belly, loud enough, painful enough to be heard.

This time, with the decision to explore being conscious during the entire process, the self actually notices the barely perceptible dripping of taste-laden saliva down the esophagus and, at the swallowing, an actual sensation she imagines as a plunk in the well of the stomach, as if a rock lands in the center of a pool. It is the feeling of the food being received.

Because the self has chosen to be conscious during this process, the plunk is very tiny. This time the food is chewed, not gulped, and there is the intention of attending to the process!

Then, there is the marked realization that the self can choose what bite to take, to please a part of the self's being! Just now, the soul itself loves the sweetness and freshness and aliveness of the shredded beet, so the self takes a bite of that to explore and enjoy more fully the sensations of eating this beet, as part of the family of Source!

Then, comes the choice to please the emotional body, so there is the selection of a bite of goat cheese, and there is a general hum and pacifying of the inner child.

With the attending comes a moment when the physical body relays to the self that it wants no more, and the rest of the salad is put aside for later.

Remarkable that all this takes place, if one attends!

No wonder the child has had no patience for eating! There was no prescription or direction in attending, for taking time to acknowledge an act of loving, nourishing, nurturing, or any sensation of pleasure in the process. There was only the attempt to feel some frantic form of comforting, and soothing, as replacement for absent mother—the mother herself frantic and overwhelmed!

Before, there had been no attending to anything past the prayer of gratitude and the first few bites. There had been little recognition at all of any involvement in the chewing or swallowing or noting of the effects on the stomach.

I know I won't do this for every meal. There isn't always the time. Or is there, if I plan it that way, if I set aside the time to care for the needs of physical, emotional, and soul bodies? Already, there is the feeling of panic if some part of me should dictate that this attending must happen at every instance of eating.

There is no need for a dictate, I hear. Instead, it is about having this awareness now, and taking the time in the future, as much as possible to grow a habit, to consciously choose what the self wants to eat in the moment, and being conscious when I eat it. I am aware that I am nurturing myself, loving myself, as I eat and taste what I eat.

This is really about attending to the child, rather than dumping a plate down in front of her and expecting her to eat—without love, or care, or attention—and feeling overwhelmed at the same time, as my mother often felt while feeding us. I am not in any way blaming her. I am, by mentioning her here, helping myself understand where these tendencies came from so that I can heal them for myself.

The simple exercise of really attending now, kinesthetically, allows the self to anchor this experience, and with every attending, when it happens, the anchor is strengthened. (Somewhat like flossing!)

The experiment continues, a closer look at the next stages.

There is the feeling, on a psychic level, of the stomach lining absorbing the nutrients and gently sending them into the blood stream, into the internal living network, to feed the cells that provide the energy for the arms, legs, torso, the brain to form thoughts and words, the mouth to speak the truths of the self.

And then, lastly, there is the flush of energy sent out like rays of the sun, from all parts of the body: the body's life force, its electrical energy, flooding the living network, returning itself to itself, a full revolution of sequence.

Thus, the individual Source Self, through collaboration of self and body, merges truly with all it has absorbed, each individual particle of nourishment, each a part of the Oneness, from beginning to end.

What a miraculous journey! The self and the body become as partners, become as one, in the system of the inner and outer living networks, the inner mirroring the outer in form of activity and living vitality.

There is a blessedness here. There is a deepening of the term *beloved*. There is a loving devotion given to every nuance, every cell, every particle of Source itself, in the study and exploration of this individual Source Self, as it humbly begins a relationship with its given body.

And there is boundless gratitude, as well as a sense of expectancy and excitement in this new awareness.

And, of course, there is more! Always!

29

THE SUBSTANCE OF JOY

February 29, 2012

This morning, I've been longing to connect with the magic in the woods, the multidimensional realm, and feeling somehow not whole, not complete without it. Do I need to go to the woods to feel the magic? Can I not be Oneness, as well as individual Source Self, in everything that I do, wherever I am?

I've been reading about the Australian aborigines and the way they live. What of their walk-abouts? Do they question what they are doing in the moment? Do they ask, what is the purpose in this? What is the import in that?

Does the deer ask this? Does the crow? The wind?

When I am both Oneness and my individual Source Self, no matter what I am doing in the moment, I am here. HERE. NOW. And that is enough.

The other day in the woods, as I sat on the log, loving where I was, enjoying the state of not thinking but just being, the question came into my mind: What do I want to do next? And I thought about that, and I began to realize the humor in it, in that question, what do I want to do next?

Who will I be in that linear "next" time? How will I know what I feel like doing when that linear "next" time comes, for it is not now. It is only now, in the now-time that I can truly say what I want to do or eat or create in the moment.

So much has been said about "the here and the now," and I am beginning to understand.

Every moment of "here" is blessed if the "I" that is my personality self, my three-dimensional self, will allow that. Every moment of "now" and "here" is already blessed by my individual Source Self, is already blessed by Source, seen and known in the multidimensional realm, accepted, hallowed, and cherished, no matter how seemingly mundane. The moment my personality self recognizes the "here" and the "now" as blessed, that self automatically slips into being Source Self. The realization of this fills me with joy.

After creating the previous chapter, I realized, as the days passed, that every particle of the living network, every nanosecond of this life that my three-dimensional body lives on this planet is part of the substance of joy.

There is so much that comes with the phrase "the substance of joy." For is that not what "here" and "now" truly are?

I talked about a plate of food that was made up of particles of beings who team together to create that which we call "food."

On a plate comprised of the earth's loving the seed, which flourished in her nurturing and became the grain that, with the assistance of a human higher mind's imagination and lower mind's development of machinery, created the harvest of grain that became the flour that created the bread cooked in the oven. The sweet cow gave her milk to be the butter to spread on the bread.

I was astounded at the idea of the magical alchemy of that entire compilation of beings along the living network, including myself, as I took that blessing into my body, as I took a bite of the substance of that joy that is the living network, that is Source itself, into the dwelling place of my body.

Am I not, dear ones, and you also, are we not all part of that substance of joy, in every living moment of the here and the now of our lives?

I do not need to walk in the woods to feel the magic. I can simply name myself here, place myself now, and notice that I am Oneness, as I am individual Source Self, here and now.

Whether I am washing my sheets, doing the dishes, hanging a picture, making a bed for a dear friend who comes next week.... Whatever I am doing, if I can welcome myself as one with the substance of joy, as part of this living network of Source itself, then I am living this magic. I am myself the magic of multidimensionality.

I AM THAT I AM. Again, we come to that. For does not being, here and now, does that not mean the same thing as the I AM THAT I AM? Am I not then Source itself simply being?

I do not need to be more. I do not need to be less. My body thanks me for this statement.

In the wealth of my being, in the wealth of my acceptance of the substance of joy that I am, there is greater joy than can be beheld by any one being at one time. It is beyond joy that I feel. It is a peacefulness, a transcendence, a rising sun of awakening. It is a feeling of rightness, in finding my place in all things.

There is merely the intention, in any one moment, to recognize myself as Oneness as well as individual Source Self, in each action, each interaction, each thought and word, even each seemingly unimportant or dreaded activity, and, immediately, there is an alchemy of my being that takes place. I want to call it "good" even though the polarities of "good" and "bad" are beginning to merge in this new era.

I look forward to this living experiment. I look forward to spending my day in this place called "here" and this time called "now." In this place of complete acceptance of every emotion that comes, every interaction that comes, every chore, every component of each chore, the gathering together of the cordless drill, the screws, the hammer, the picture hangers—whatever is involved.

I look forward to the experiment of honoring the moment in the substance of joy that I am living and breathing and sharing with the entire living network of the family of Source, as a member of that family.

The sun shines on my face through the window, sparkles on the snow. I feel its warmth, as I feel the warmth of the fire made of the sweet logs from the loving trees that offered themselves to feed me in warmth this winter.

And I thank them.

I thank the sun. I thank the wind that sends the air to create the fire in the wood.

I thank the lower mind that gathered the list of materials to make this channeling. And I thank my high heart mind, for being here and now, for hearing the wind and the chimes and the murmur and crackle of the fire as it burns, and the sound currents in my ear, notifying me of others listening, invisible others listening, here with me now.

I feel my belly supporting this laptop, into which I channel. And my belly also is a part of this living network, as I am.

I feel the sun shining through my physical eyelids, as I feel Source itself shining out of me, through me, to the stars on the other side of this planet that are invisible now—because the sun is shining—and yet I see them, through my etheric eyes, my Source Self's eyes.

There is no fear here.

There is the peace of being one with this living network. There is a thrill and joy that I share this experience with many in this moment. There is the gladness of the realization that others know this and have found this before me. There is a feeling of kindred spirit, not of competition but of community.

I feel the ever-spreading waves of that community passing across the planet in the ethers that wrap around her, just above her surface. I feel the waves of that community reaching down beneath the earth to connect with the beneath-the-earth people. I feel the angelic realm and the masters, nodding, smiling, welcoming, as they are also part of this living network.

My hands tingle with the "reconnective healing"[17] energy of the universe. It is different from other energy I have felt in my hands. I have called it "reconnective healing" because it has been labeled so, before me, and helped me to recognize this feeling that has newly come to me.

Colors come through now, many colors. They too are part of the living network. All the colors of joy. I cannot name them, they are so many and so diverse. There is a kaleidoscope of colors that I see with my etheric eyes.

There is so much here that it is a feast to my entire being. To even contemplate the ingestion of this feast is to partake of the substance of joy. And the greatest joy for me is to know, in all of my being, that I am this substance of joy, as I am that which is all around me. There is no division. There is no boundary, separation, or differentness.

And yet I am individual. In my individuality, I feel the sensations of all that I describe.

There is an absolutely beautiful peace here.

A few days ago, I told a friend that I felt as if I rested in a gossamer nest of angelic threads. They were gossamer threads comprised of the individual hairs of angels' wing feathers, woven into a soft, shimmering, crystalline nest.

I realize that it is my soul that rests in this nest, as I experience a luscious freedom to be in this here, in this now, that is the substance of joy, that is the multidimensional living network of Source itself. There is such a profound surprise to feel this freedom of being the Oneness, and also individual Source Self.

In this freedom, I honor the moment of now. I honor my individual desire to do what I want in the moment. Whatever that is, if I honor it, it suddenly becomes a multidimensional experience, for in doing so I am Source honoring the moment of my individual Source Self.

This new awareness brings me to a place that names all moments, all experiences in the living network, as a part of the substance of joy. There is even delight at the idea of feeling guilt in an interaction with another. This guilt then is something to be studied, is a tool for higher learning, a substance of joy.

A moment of shame, in an interaction with another, can also be a place of learning, bringing delight in the anticipation of learning more. This learning then becomes another ingredient of joy added to the living network of Source, for its wealth and evolution.

I find myself in this moment looking forward with a feeling of expectancy to all moments of the here and the now, a long string of them going far into the future. If I can see every moment as I live it, as part of the school of higher learning that adds to this living network, adds to the substance of joy that I am, then is there not a reason for this expectancy and excitement?

There is much to learn and experience on this path. I feel so much excitement in this moment.

I feel the pulsing expectancy of every infinitesimal particle of this living network, like tiny sea anemones moved by the current. It's an expectancy that new material and information are coming, are on their way, in every breath of each individual Source Self, as each adds to the Oneness, moment to moment, in each and every lifetime, each and every dimension and plane, knowing that this is the divine plan.

There is a buzz, a loud chatter of Morse code, of encoding, passing through the living network right now, as we speak.

I, the channel, do not know who is speaking. It does not matter. I believe it is the living network itself, in its excitement at this sharing.

There is so much information being passed at this moment, so much information now.

In the telling of these moments, there is an awakening of the collective consciousness, increasing the frequencies now moving across the living network. I take a moment to just feel this, as I ask for you readers to do also.

It may be that you sense it, in your imaginations. It may be that you sense it as a sensation in your body, or that you sense nothing at all. Know, dear ones, that you do feel it, on some level. And know that, as I have said before, as you intend it, so does it happen.

Allow yourselves now to become truly a part of this living network, as you step into the here and the now of being Oneness at the same time as being your individual Source Self.

Allow this now. Allow the alchemy of this moment. Step into this moment, as you take this moment into yourself.

Name yourself part of the substance of joy.

Name yourself I AM THAT I AM.

Say the words to yourself: I AM HERE. I AM NOW.

I AM ONENESS, AS I AM INDIVIDUAL SOURCE SELF, NOW, AND HERE.

I AM THE LIVING NETWORK. I AM THE SUBSTANCE OF JOY.

I AM THAT I AM.

Allow the expectancy and the excitement of the experience of all emotions, all interactions, all creations, as they happen.

Be a part of this living experiment.

Be a part of this living experience.

Feel yourselves surrounded by the masters, the angelic realm, the Oneness, and feel yourself as a part of this living network, dear ones. And if there come times when you forget, know that, even your forgetting is a part of the experience. Simply remind yourself: I am here. This is now. Or if you'd like, allow yourself to learn from whatever experience has taken you away from that "here" and "now." Do not judge that time. Do not judge that experience.

Know that every fragment, every particle of your living adds information and wealth to the substance of joy, to the living network, and Source itself—and therefore, you.

My master self and the masters add: *Blessings, dear ones.*

We cherish each and every one of you on your path.

You are beloved of us.

There is much gratitude here, for every facet of your existence, every facet of your living, being, breathing, here on this planet.

Thank you, beloved readers.

We wish you expectancy and excitement with all of the possibilities before you.

Go in peace, dear ones.

Go in peace.

What quality of joy!
I can't help but say, *Thank you!*

30

ALTARS TO THE BELOVEDS

January 30, 2014

I moved two more times after last writing for this book, although I started other books during that time. I needed to put this away for a while so I could find the true voice of it, make it shine, and give honor to its closure. I needed to place it in the ordering of my life.

I believe I have at last found home, again here in Colrain, but it doesn't matter what house I live in. What matters is that where I live is an altar, always, as I am.

I am an altar to the Beloved that is Source. Every step of my path places itself on the altar of my soul's devotion. Each thought I have, each prayer, each dream, each teaching, every moment of anguish, despair, hope, joy, is a crystal of experience that I offer with humility and intention to humanity's unfolding.

I surround myself with altars of crystals and stones and shells, feathers and bones, and visible fragments of my soul's three-dimensional path on this planet in this lifetime. I place each object as I place each step, attending to its alignment with the vibrations of my soul. When an object or a step does not feel right, I change it.

Each particle of joy, love, guilt, shame, rightness, truth—every strength, every weakness, I place before you, my reader. You are my witness. I am student and teacher. I am wise woman and tiny child. I am human endeavoring to evolve myself, as I endeavor to assist in my small way in humanity's evolution.

My mother died exactly five years ago today. When I began this book, I was searching for ways to learn to love myself, to build within me a divine mother—the divine feminine—which I felt I knew little about. I began by asking the masters, not trusting myself to know. As I explored and developed the loving mother within, I began to build and trust my own wisdom. I began to expand my ability to sense and see and hear the multidimensional realm in which I live. I opened myself to being more fully present in consciousness and began to trust my master self.

I experienced being held in the mother darkness, that dark, fathomless well of silence and safety, mystery and enchantment, where dwells a love of such gentleness and such devotion that, even now, it fills me and moves me to tears, as I call it forth.

I have begun to have a relationship with my body and I am deeply grateful for that. I have learned so much, yet there is still so much to learn.

I thank my readers for inspiring me. Know that wherever you are on your path, it is exactly right. Know that whatever you place on the altar of your soul's devotion is received with awe, love and gratitude.

Allow these words to move through you, whisper the masters. *Know that they spark and activate your soul in its own evolution. Allow yourself this initiation. Place yourself as an altar to the beloved that you are, and see yourself as a crystalline structure of transformation.*

With all grace and devotion, we send to you our gratitude and love for all that you do, in the name of your own evolution which is the evolution of all.

As you intend it, so does it happen.

In the name of Source and the beloved that you are, dear ones, go in peace.

Go in peace.

EPILOGUE

My beloved Yeshu and I, Magdalen, stand in a sea of crystals at the central altar of the Temple of the Beloved.

We await one who is beloved to us.

We have shared more than lifetimes with her.

We have lived through her and she, through us.

There are times when we have been one and the same, and other times when we were separate but always joined in love.

There have been many initiations over the lifetimes in Egypt, Tibet, Alexandria, Britain, Greece, on Venus and other planets, and other places on this planet that we are not given to name, that she remembers. Other initiations she has forgotten.

This initiation is different. In this lifetime now, she is embodied, incarnate, and we are of the ethers, sitting with the masters that we are, and only seen by those who can truly see, only heard by those who can truly hear.

We await her, in this temple. And she comes now. The double outer doors open to bright sunlight for a moment, and she—the honored one—enters. Then, the doors close to candlelight again.

She wears a long, white flowing gown. Her arms are bare. Her feet are bare. There is a white blindfold covering her eyes, and she is led by two novices, young girls.

They lead her slowly, gently, with the solemnity of ritual, through the outer chamber, stepping to either side of her as she walks on a path of blood-red rose petals strewn thickly on the floor beneath her feet. It is the path of the mother darkness, the rich deep red of the first blood of the innocent, the uninitiated.

Her tread is regal and, at the same time, she is full of awe at the honor of being included in this ritual of the ancient mysteries. Her blindfold becomes wet with tears that seep through and stream down her cheeks.

She is deeply moved.

From where we stand, separate from and unseen by the other initiates, Yeshu and I smell the attar of roses. We smell her particular scent in recognition. We smile to each other and grasp each other's hands for a moment in our joy at this reunion with her and in our excitement in her initiation.

As she nears the doors to the inner temple, her blindfold is removed. She catches her breath as she sees us, and the tears of her joy almost blind her completely. We watch her whole being as the part of her that yearns to reach out to us gives way to the part that knows she must attend.

She is led to the circle of waiting initiates, like and unlike her. She sits in the chair shown to her, with the other initiates also seated, in a circle around the altar of crystals where we stand unseen by the others.

She is barely aware of the others. She barely sees them. She looks straight into our eyes, hers full of curiosity at our presence, and also deep devotion, love, and such gratitude that we feel it, all of it, in our etheric hearts.

She watches us, her eyes getting rounder, as we move now to stand at her feet. And then we kneel there, and she emits a cry, a bellow of grief, surprise, dumbfounded joy beyond belief, love beyond any measure possible, as we each, Yeshu and I, gently take one of her feet into our hands. We place her feet in a bowl of warm, rose-scented water, and we begin to lovingly wash them, and anoint them in oil, only her feet, this beloved, so dear to us.

She has no words.

She is more than deeply moved.

Her face is wet with tears, again, of joy, astonishment, and humility. She smiles, her soul in her eyes. She knows that she is home, that we are home to her, the masters are home to her, and she belongs here with us, in this temple.

She is also aware, just barely, that she sits in a circle of other initiates, that she has work to do here on this planet, incarnate here in this lifetime.

When her name is called to go into the initiation chamber, when the novices appear to lead her there, she knows with absolute cer-

tainty—in her heart and in her soul—that we remain with her, always. In this way, she knows that she belongs always, wherever she is.

Long before this initiation, before the mists of linear time, when Source was barely a whisper in the realm of that which this initiate has called the Hidden Source—without any consciousness of itself—there is a trace of memory shared between us, the initiate and I, of that realm of the unspoken, the unrevealed, the unseen, the unknown.

At that time, the initiate and I were one.

One might say that all were one at that time, but it is not so that all share conscious memory of it. We have, as one, the memory in our cells, of the time when Source became conscious, when Source's desire to know and be known was born. We share the moment of the Divine Arc Welder's sparks in the Flame of Creation, when each individual Source Self began its path as a Beloved.

At that time, as I have said, the initiate and I were one, shared conscious memory. Yet, embedded within our shared monad were the seeds of the souls of each of us and many others, each soul tracking its path back to that time of the Flame of Creation itself.

So it was that I knew and remember that, in the very moment of her individual soul seed's formation, this initiate received what she sensed were two words spoken under the breath of Source, faint as a whisper or an echo, without conscious language or thought and yet immediately embedded into her etheric cells.

She carried the thread of these words across all her existence, across her soul's lineage of lifetimes, on every step of the path she *took as a beloved from Source back to Source, through all the planes and levels and dimensions of her destiny.*

And it is now, in the moment that she steps across this threshold into this initiation chamber, that all gather—all lifetimes, all steps, all thresholds, all initiation chambers become one. It is only now that she is meant to hear what the breath of Source whispered so long ago, so that she may live them for herself.

The two words of Source, as spoken to all its creation and yet deeply embedded into this initiate's very being were "eternal vow."

Yeshu and I watch as the mists of this initiation clear and return the initiate to this time, this place, now, the next part of her path before her. We sit beside her as she watches the sun slip behind the mountain, its cosmic ball of fire showing like flashing lights, sparks, just for a moment through the bare winter trees of the mountain top, before it begins a new path to a new dawn.

NOTES

1. Leonardo da Vinci's *La Scapigliata* (circa 1500), drawing on paper, Galleria Nazionale of Parma, Italy. The cover image is an adaptation of the original, "by grant of the Ministry of heritage, cultural activities and tourism - the National Gallery of Parma" (wording here specified by the museum). Please go to the last page in the book for more about the cover.
2. *Wikipedia,* s.v. "Psalm 23."
3. Brooks, *Love Incarnate: I have come to tell a story of love.*
4. Ibid., 198-199.
5. Robinson, *Nag Hadammi Library In English*, *Gospel of Mary (BG8502,1), 523-527.* The Berlin Codex (also known as the Akhmim Codex), given the accession number Papyrus Berolinensis 8502, is a Coptic manuscript from the 5th century AD, per Wikipedia.com.

6. Ibid., 525. The actual quote is as follows: "Mary answered and said, 'What is hidden from you I will proclaim to you.'"
7. Brooks, *Love Incarnate*, 73.
8. Ibid., 184-189.
9. Ibid., 123-130.
10. Michelangelo Buonarroti's *Pieta* (1498-99), marble, can be viewed at the Basilica of St Peter, The Vatican, Rome, Italy.
11. The School of the Golden Discs, run by Zayne and Moriah Marston, is located in Colrain, MA. The website for the school is: www.transformationaltimes.com.

    Moriah Marston channels the Tibetan ascended master known as Djwhal Khul.
12. Co-founder of The School of the Golden Discs (see note 11).
13. As channeled through Moriah Marston.
14. *Webster's Ninth New Collegiate Dictionary*, s.v. "glyph."
15. Brooks, *Love Incarnate*, 1.
16. *Webster's Ninth New Collegiate Dictionary*, s.v. "mirabile dictu," means *"wonderful to relate."*
17. Pearl, *The Reconnection*.
18. *Wikipedia*, s.v. "Catharism."
19. Ibid., s.v. "Goddess of Willendorf."
20. Bethards, *The Dream Book*, 126.
21. Transformationaltimes.com, s.v. "The Tibetan."

22. Hartman, *Young America Sings*, 12.
23. *Wikipedia*, s.v. "*La Scapigliata.*"

GLOSSARY

References here to specific books can be found in the Selected Bibliography following.

AKASHIC RECORDS. These refer to all of the records of the soul, since its inception as a monad of Source—past, present, future, parallel lifetimes, backwards and forwards to the divine plan of the soul—including all details, as stored in the archives in the fifth dimensional (causal) plane.

ARCHANGELS. Each archangel has his or her own specialty, and it is wonderful to call on them for assistance. Any individual archangel mentioned in the text is listed by name alphabetically below.

ASCENDED MASTER. Please see my descriptions on page xv, as well as page 19. For further details on individual masters, there are several websites devoted entirely to their duties and descriptions. For instance, see www.soundofheart.org. Every piece of channeled information always comes through the individual filter of the channeler so take what works for you and leave what doesn't.

BLEED-THROUGH EXPERIENCE. This means living in the present as well as feeling sensations, whether physical or psychic, and/or emotions from a different time, this life or another.

BRIDGE CHAKRA. For many years, I have felt the etheric presence of what I call a "bridge chakra," which bridges the chakras at the heart and solar plexus. Other healers and teachers that I know have also noticed the presence of this chakra.

CATHARS. "Catharism…was a Christian dualist movement that thrived in some areas of Southern Europe, particularly northern Italy and southern France, between the 12th and 14th centuries…. The Inquisition was established in 1234 to uproot the remaining Cathars."[18] See the *Select Bibliography* for direction to read more about them.

CAUSAL BODY. The soul body.

CHAKRA. A portal in the aura of the body, which allows energy to enter and leave. The seven main chakras are (from bottom to top): the root chakra at the base of the spine; the (what I call) spleen chakra or second chakra in the belly;

the solar plexus or third chakra in the high crook of the rib cage; the heart or fourth chakra over the thymus gland in the chest; the throat or fifth chakra in the throat; the third eye or sixth chakra at the forehead; and the crown or seventh chakra at the top of the head.

CHANNELING. This is defined on p. xvii, in the Introduction.

CORDS. Often when we think of people over and over again, or if we shoot anger at them over and over again, or in any constant flow of energy, we create a traveled path of energy, called a "cord" which keeps us energetically connected to those people, whether we like it or not. This is much like a dirt road in mud season when the more one travels the same ruts, the deeper they embed, so one cannot help but end up traveling in the same one or two ruts.

DEVAS. These are like faeries. Each flower has its own deva, a nature spirit who protects as well as has specific healing properties of that particular plant. For more on this, see *Plant Spirit Medicine* by Eliot Cowan.

DIVINE MASCULINE. (See also pp. 205-209 in the text.) In addition, I have compiled a list here of the qualities that I see as aspects of the divine masculine. They include clarity, discernment, action, doing, thinking, creating, formulating, manifesting, directing, planning, analyzing, and others.

EGO-SYNTONIC. This means in alignment with the ego. Ego-dystonic means at odds with the ego, or against its grain.

ELEMENTALS. These are the beings of the elements. They are, to me, something like faeries in that they have personalities, thoughts, wishes, and lives of their own.

ENSOULMENT. Living as soul in body.

ETHERIC. Anything of the ethers. For example, the aura is of the etheric plane. Etheric fingers are the fingers made up of the energy of the aura surrounding the physical fingers. Etheric ears are the aura's ears or the soul's ears, since the soul lives in the etheric plane, rather than the physical three-dimension, visible plane.

FIFTH DIMENSION. The dimension in which it is said that the soul lives, although I believe that the soul can experience all dimensions, as it is multidimensional.

FORCE FIELD. Our energy field, or aura. Try the exercise of letting people stand some distance away from you and then have them walk closer and see when you can feel them in your field. THAT is your force field. The size of it differs among people.

GODDESS OF WILLENDORF. "Now known in academia as the Woman of Willendorf, is a 4.25-inch (10.8 cm) high statuette of a female figure estimated to have been made between about 28,000 and 25,000 BCE… (It) is named after the site in Austria where it was unearthed…."[19]

I AM THAT I AM. This is God, Source, each of us when we are, quite simply, in the all of who we are, in pure beingness.

There is no judgment here, no ego, nothing outside of who I am fully in my Sourceness, or Oneness.

INTERGALACTIC FAMILIES. These are all the beings in the universes, of whom we are all family, as part of the family of Source.

INTROJECTION. The opposite of projection. To introject is to unconsciously take on the feelings or attitudes of another. To project is to unconsciously put out onto another one's own feelings or attitudes.

KARMA. Intentions, thoughts, and actions in one or several lifetimes combine to block or enhance the soul's path to its highest evolution. Only through working through the issues represented by these blocks can the path be cleared for further advancement. There is a definite quality of cause and effect at play here.

KUNDALINI. "Life force, spiritual power, Holy Spirit, God energy; housed in the spine and awakens seven chakras to full potential."[20] I see it as a flame of Source's creative energy spiraling up the chakras from the earth through the root to the crown and up, connecting us to the magic of the universes, once awakened.

LADY GAIA. The ascended master who is the personality of the Planet Earth.

LAWS OF ATTRACTION. The more you think of something, the more you attract that same something to yourself.

MAGICAL CHILD. The original pure child inside who has access to all of her divine creativity, magic, and delight.

MICHAEL. This is Archangel Michael who vanquishes "evil" or "dark" energy. He has legions of armies that assist him in this.

MONAD. The product of the first splitting of Source into myriad parts, further splitting into the souls that we are. Some believe that each monad then splits into multiple "oversouls" which then split again into multiple souls. There are different theories involved here, as I believe that the high self is directly connected to the soul. If curious, do explore further.

MULTIDIMENSIONALITY. Defined on p. xviii.

PLANETARY LOGOS. I see the planetary logos as the ascended master or masters who think/feel/love/orchestrate the planet into creation. See also Janet McClure's book in the *Select Bibliography*.

QUAN YIN. Chinese Buddhist deity embodying loving kindness and compassion.

RAPHAEL. The Archangel Raphael whose specialty is all manners of healing. Raphael especially loves to be called.

ST. GERMAINE. This ascended master was once Merlin and also Christopher Columbus, among some of the lifetimes he lived. He specializes in transformation and magic. See Godfré Ray King's *Unveiled Mysteries*.

THE TIBETAN (DJHWAL KHUL). The Tibetan is, as Moriah Marston says, "one of the Ascended Masters who is recognized as the 'great psychologist' and teacher of higher metaphysical laws."[21] Alice Bailey is best known for channeling the Tibetan, but Moriah Marston makes his message more easily accessible.

VYWAMUS. An ascended master who has never been incarnated (in body) and who is the higher self of Sanat Kumara, the planetary logos (creator) of the Planet Earth. Sanat Kumara and Sonanda are one and the same. Vywamus loves to assist in channeling.

SELECT BIBLIOGRAPHY

Baigent, Michael, Richard Leigh, and Henry Lincoln. *Holy Blood, Holy Grail*. New York: Dell publishing, 1983. This is an excellent resource for information about the Knights Templar who championed the Cathars.

Bethards, Betty. *The Dream Book: Symbols for Self Understanding*. Petaluma: New Century Publishers, 2012.

Brooks, Leslie. *Love Incarnate: I have come to tell a story of love*. Colrain: Love Incarnate Books, 2009.

Burnham, Sophy. *The Treasure of Montségur: A Novel of the Cathars*. San Francisco: Harper Collins, 2002.

Cowan, Eliot. *Plant Spirit Medicine: The Healing Power of Plants*. Columbus: Swan-Raven & Company, 1995.

Hartman, Dennis, Editor. *Young America Sings*. Los Angeles: National Poetry Press, 1969.

Hughes, Nita, *Past Recall: When Love and Wisdom Transcend Time*. Tacoma: Pyradice Publishing, 2003. I bought this book along with *The Cathar Legacy* from a little bookshop in France when I visited the ruins of Montségur which was one of the last strongholds of the Cathars.

Hughes, Nita. *The Cathar Legacy*. Tacoma: Pyradice Publishing, 2006.

King, Godfré Ray. *Unveiled Mysteries*. Charleston: BiblioBazaar, 2007.

Longfellow, Ki. *The Secret Magdalene*. Brattleboro: Eio Books, 2005. I include this book here because it is my favorite book of all time. A profound read.

McClure, Janet (Channel for Vywamus). *The Story of Sanat Kumara, Training a Planetary Logos*. Sedona: Light Technology Publishing and Printing, 1990.

Pearl, Eric. *The Reconnection*. Carlsbad: Hay House, 2011.

Robinson, James N., General Editor. *Nag Hadammi Library In English* (New York: Harper Collins, 1990), *Gospel of Mary (BG8502,1), 523—527*.

Webster's Ninth New Collegiate Dictionary. Springfield: Merriam-Webster Inc., 1988.

ABOUT THE AUTHOR

Leslie Brooks has a bachelors degree in art with a minor in poetry, a masters degree in counseling psychology, an advanced certification in Heart-centered hypnotherapy,™ and is a Master RoHun Therapist. She took her first color class at the age of five, her art has shown in several museums across the country, and she was first published in a national anthology of poetry[22] at the age of sixteen.

Her first love is writing her soul, which is precious to her. Otherwise, she loves nature, working in her flower gardens, and playing with friends.

Leslie lives in Western Massachusetts with the birds, deer, beavers, porcupines, foxes, and faeries.

Her website is www.love-incarnate.com.

ABOUT THE COVER

I would like to share a little more information about *La Scapigliata*. Per Wikipedia, "The work is an unfinished painting, mentioned for the first time in the House of Gonzaga collection in 1627. It is perhaps...a Madonna.... The painting, part of the Parmesan collection since 1839, has been dated to Leonardo's mature period, near to the *Virgin of the Rocks* or *The Virgin and Child with St Anne and St. John the Baptist*."[23]

Also, it was really quite an extraordinary experience retrieving the image itself from the museum in Italy. I had emailed the museum in the broken Italian I had learned on my trip to Italy with my ex-husband in 1983, but received no response from them so I just assumed it wasn't going to happen.

Months later, after I'd given up on the idea, an email arrived from Italy, from the archives department of the museum, all in Italian of course, and I couldn't understand a word other than the subject. I panicked for a moment then found a translation site online, we wrote back and forth, all in Italian, and got all the details and payment worked out. I had my bank wire them the euros to pay for the image, and then one day, I received the image itself.

I cannot tell you, my readers, what a thrill it was to see the digital photograph taken from the actual drawing done by Leonardo da Vinci in the 1500s. The horizontal striations are the original paper. I somehow feel as if I have touched the work itself and thus the master, and he lives through the work, and has become a part of my work here.